TANYA'S
Christmas

Published by Blink Publishing
3.08, The Plaza,
535 Kings Road,
Chelsea Harbour,
London, SW10 0SZ

www.blinkpublishing.co.uk

facebook.com/blinkpublishing
twitter.com/blinkpublishing

Hardback – 978-1-911-600-41-1
Signed edition – 978-1-788-700–15–3
Ebook – 978-1-911-600-48-0

A CIP catalogue of this book is available from the British Library.

Printed and bound in Italy

1 3 5 7 9 10 8 6 4 2

Publisher: Kelly Ellis
Project Editor: Laura Herring
Creative Editor: Lucy Brazier
Designed by Emily Rough
Food stylist: Alexandra Heaton
Food props stylist: Victoria Allen
Christmas stylists: House of Bunting

Blink Publishing is an imprint of the Bonnier Publishing Group
www.bonnierpublishing.co.uk

TANYA'S Christmas

TANYA BURR

BLINK
bringing you closer

Contents

The Christmas Spirit

'Twas the night before Christmas, when all through the house not a creature was stirring. Well, apart from Mum and Dad frantically wrapping – lost in a flurry of ribbon curls and paper. The stockings were hung by the chimney with care and my sister and I sat in matching pyjamas watching The Muppet Christmas Carol. *We knew we should be nestled snugly in our beds because the sooner we were asleep, the sooner we would wake up and HE would have been! Overwhelmed by tiredness, we headed to bed and dreamt of star-filled skies and a crimson sleigh pulled by dancing reindeers…*

These are the memories that come to me when I reflect on the childhood excitement of Christmases past. Christmas has been my favourite time of year for as long as I can remember. I'm forever grateful to my parents for making it such a special time, and for creating traditions that live on beyond my childhood. I'll never forget the feeling of waking up at 6am on Christmas morning to a lumpy stocking filled with presents. But it was never just about the gifts. My love for Christmas stems from its customs and spirit – and from the anticipation it brings. When I was tiny I had a *Ladybird* book about Baby Jesus and the Nativity and I knew it off by heart before I could read. It's amazing to truly believe in the wonder of Christmas and, now that I'm older, I love watching the children in my family have the same enchanting experience.

I still believe in that magic and being a grown-up has not spoilt that. In fact, it is just as thrilling to share my love for the season and create some of the magic for those around me. Someone once tweeted me: 'Watching your videos, even when they have nothing to do with Christmas, makes me feel Christmassy!' Another tweeted, saying: 'I can't wait for you to start uploading Christmas videos, you are the one person I rely on to get me in the festive mood!' I always have a wonderful response from my followers at Christmas time and those messages make me feel like one of Santa's elves whose job it is to get people in the mood for the festivities. That's a rather lovely

job to have. I thought that writing a book all about Christmas would be the most wonderful project and hopefully something you will all enjoy and find useful.

I still get that same joy each year when I start to see the festive holiday signs: tubs of *Quality Street* appearing in the supermarkets; drinking my coffee from a *Starbucks* seasonal red cup; watching *Elf* for the first time in December; seeing the bright Christmas lights and snow-decorated shop window displays; and catching the *Coca Cola* advert on TV. Christmas time combines my favourite things in life, like baking, spending time with loved ones, parties, cosy nights in and surprises! It brings with it a unique, captivating feeling like no other time of year and I want to capture that here in these pages.

So much of December focuses on social events and it's another reason why this month is so special to me. I love going out with my husband Jim and my friends, or inviting people over for our annual big party, or for dinner. There is always a Girls' Night In and often a friend joining me for an evening of baking and crafting. I have written about this in my first chapter as well as the joy and importance of taking time out from the busy season and heading to the sofa to recharge my batteries: PJs, film, hot chocolate (sometimes with a dash of *Baileys*!) and my pup snuggled at my feet.

Now, as you probably know, I'm a real home-maker so I love to fill every room in the house with a warm yuletide glow. I am eager to share my interior tips for the season and some simple homemade ways to make your space feel welcoming and festive.

I am a big believer that fairy lights and a little DIY can transform anyone's home, so let's get creative! By the time you have finished reading this book, I hope to have inspired you to feel more festive than ever, with your home sparklingly ready for family and friends to gather and Father Christmas to come down the chimney.

Speaking of guests, I adore hosting a Christmas party. It is one of my favourite things to do at this time of year. I know it can be daunting, but trust me, with a bit of organisation, it's a lot of fun. I will share with you quick, easy and foolproof party food and cocktail recipes. I'll also share some ideas for the perfect outfit and makeup, as well as a playlist to guarantee you have a merry time. The great thing about December is how quickly we can all get into the spirit. Throwing a party isn't about perfection or expense, and you don't need to worry about fancy canapés and entertainment. What everyone really wants is a fun celebration, a good vibe where you can chat, dance, eat mince pies, drink mulled wine and sing along to the King of Christmas, Michael Bublé. I also wanted this book to be bursting with gift ideas and instructions for crafts and activities: from wreath-making to creating your own tealight holders and scented decorations, and from beauty treatments to sewing your own advent calendar. You can create clever displays and decorations with the simplest tools and a bit of glittery vision. Presents can be homemade too (often the best ones are), so I have included some that never fail to win hearts, as well as

definitive gift-buying ideas for those close to you, with extra attention paid to Secret Santa! I couldn't miss out present-wrapping tips and budget-friendly solutions, too. Did you know Champagne can be cheaper in December than any other time of the year?!

As you know from my baking videos and previous book, *Tanya Bakes*, baking is a huge part of my life and even more so at Christmas time. So my recipes take pride of place in this book, in a chapter of their own as well as dotted elsewhere throughout the pages. There are many of my favourite festive recipes with traditional dishes like mince pies (page 158) and my Christmas Lunch (pages 206–18) with the essential timings, plus some modern twists on Christmas baking and cocktails! To me, there is nothing better than dancing around the kitchen to Wizzard's 'I Wish It Could Be Christmas Every Day', while making an enormous batch of Gingerbread Cupcakes (page 156) that fill the house with that classic, Christmas scent.

I couldn't write this book without sharing with you some of my private family revelries over the festive break, including how we spend the special time between Christmas and New Year, when everyone and everything slows down. I love reconnecting with my family and those I don't get to see regularly. Sometimes it's not just about celebrating the holiday but surviving it too, and it's important for us all to take time out. Particularly as we approach the new year. It's a great time to reflect, be grateful, recognise the difficult bits of the year passed and think about what we want to achieve going forward. Maybe to think in terms of intentions rather than resolutions.

My wish for you all is to have the most wonderful Christmas imaginable, and I hope this book helps that happen and becomes your go-to book for festive inspiration and guidance, not just for this Christmas but for all those magical ones to come.

It's beginning to look a lot like Christmas…

Love, Tanya x

December, 1994

CHAPTER ONE
Embrace Your Inner Elf

❧ Embrace Your Inner Elf ❧

As a big fan of Christmas you would think it would be easy for me to achieve that Christmassy feeling, but even I have to actively seek it out. I think it is important to start as soon as December does, so don't delay – plan some adventures to get into the spirit. There are only 24 days until The Big One and they fly by. The anticipation of Christmas can be as thrilling as the actual event itself. I want you to get every last drop of festive enjoyment from the month and make the most of seasonal recipes, wardrobe, makeup and fairy lights.

I find the best way to kick-start the month is with a good, old-fashioned list. You may know I am an obsessive list-maker for all sorts of situations, and I probably write more than I should, but I can honestly say that when it comes to December I would be lost without one. My list covers all the main subjects like presents, food, crafts, party planning and styling, and this book is full of my tips and inspiration for all those areas.

Whether you are list writing, party planning, crafting or baking, make sure you keep the Christmas spirit alive. Pop on your festive playlist or an iconic Christmas film and have a plate of something delicious to hand, like a pile of my Iced, Spiced Scones (page 148). Setting the scene is crucial to getting in the mood, so I have included my Top Ten lists of films and books, too (pages 23 and 231). My Christmas doesn't really get under way until I have watched *Elf*!

I'll confess, I am an early tree buyer. I want to have the longest possible time to enjoy the magic it brings into the house along with all the gorgeous decorations, collected and homemade, that I adorn it with. In fact, the whole house is decorated during the first week of December in time for my Girls' Night In, my annual Christmas party, and to enjoy throughout the month. More of this in Chapter 2, where I share my styling tips and inspiration for decking your halls.

In the early days of the month I love heading into the city to enjoy the illuminations, do some window shopping (Selfridges, Liberty and Harrods put on the most extravagant displays!) and meet a friend for my favourite *Starbucks* Salted Caramel Hot Chocolate or a cocktail after work. Often, local towns and cities make a big event of switching on their Christmas lights; there is an impromptu street market with entertainment and the shops stay open late. It's a great way of soaking up the atmosphere without the last-minute shopping panic.

One of the best things about the holiday is spending some of it with those I love. Go to parties or throw your own! Say yes to all the lovely social invitations you get but remember to leave a little time throughout the month to be quiet and cosy at home. There is nothing worse than getting to Christmas Eve feeling tired, jaded and unable to look at another mince pie or glass of fizz. It's all about balance and I have to constantly remind myself of this as I get over-excited and think I can do it all.

Throughout this book I talk about my own traditions and how much that has shaped my Christmases past and present. I was lucky to grow up in a family who love Christmas, with parents who created the most amazing celebrations over the years. One of my earliest memories of the festive build-up was the arrival of The Christmas Box. My mum would go to the local supermarket and find the biggest empty cardboard box to bring home. Over the weeks leading up to Christmas she would add extra treats to her usual weekly shop: a tube of *Pringles*, Medjool dates, bags of nuts, our favourite *Cheesy Puffs* and always a large tin (no plastic tubs in those days) of *Quality Street* that would be added to the box. I can still remember the anticipation and delight of peering in and watching the pile of goodies grow each week. I was never ever tempted to delve in early!

As well as my own traditions, I am keen to include new ones that can become our Christmas celebrations of the future. I love finding out how you all choose to celebrate and getting inspiration from each of you. With that in mind, I asked my

fans across the globe to tell me about their best loved traditions and the response was incredible. There was a *Twitter* frenzy and I just knew I had to share some of them here in this book (pages 28–9) – a big, warm thank you to all of you who responded!

So, embrace your inner elf and dispel the Grinch that lurks in the shadows. It's time to work on that Christmas cheer, say yes to ice skating and buy a new pair of festive socks for snug evenings at home.

Where To Go and What To Do

Going out in December feels like stepping into an instant celebration. Everywhere buzzes with festivity – music, an abundance of pretty lights, opulent decorations and people in party mode. It sets the tone and it doesn't take much for me to be completely in the moment, whatever my plans are.

There are lots of activities I love to do this month and top of my list is ice skating. From November onwards, temporary rinks pop up across the country, so be brave and get those ice skates on. I took my mum and brother to the rink outside the Natural History Museum one year. I was very nervous but one of the staff was so lovely and gave me confidence to give it a go. Don't forget to book your slot and make sure you are properly kitted out – it's a great excuse to wear your bobble hat, scarf and glove combination!

Check what is on in your local area, because lots of venues create the most amazing themed events, trails and grottos where there could be an appearance from the Big

Man himself. It's brilliant to take the younger ones in your family too, and seeing their delight just fuels your own. Steam trains and trams are turned into *The Polar Express* for the holiday, complete with singing waiters. The most renowned Winter Wonderland is the spectacular attraction in London's Hyde Park, which is free to enter so you can just go along for a festive wander or take advantage of all the entertainment.

When I was little we would go to the carol concert at our village church and the local pantomime every year – both are good outings to do with the entire family. Ballet is traditional at Christmas and completely magical, so if you get the chance to go, make sure you see 'The Nutcracker'. I also couldn't wait for whatever the latest Christmas film release was and still make time for a trip to the cinema before the holiday. Keep an eye out for outdoor roof-top cinemas showing festive classics – what could be better than sitting under the stars, nestled in blankets and sipping a hot chocolate?

As much as I love shopping, it can easily become more of a chore than a pleasure in December. One way of avoiding this is to spend the day in the magical surroundings of an outdoor Christmas market. It's a great way to find unique gifts from small producers, sample delicious artisan food and support small local businesses.

Walking around the wooden chalet stalls with mittened hands clasping a steaming cup of mulled wine, surrounded by the aroma of Christmas and handcrafted decorations always inspires me. You don't have to travel as far afield as Europe when you can head to Birmingham (which hosts the largest German market outside of the country). Other Christmas markets with a great reputation include Bath, London's Southbank, Edinburgh, Belfast, Manchester and Cardiff.

One of my favourite things to do during the run-up to Christmas is a craft workshop, as I love learning a new skill. If you have always fancied making your own Christmas cards, decorations and gifts, there are lots of ideas to choose from. I was so proud of the wreath I made once that I have included instructions on how you can make your very own (page 64).

It's important to create fun-filled memories and embrace the clichés!

I love to eat out and one of my most memorable Christmas party dinners was with my amazing work team, Lucy, Georgia and Kate, at London's indulgent Soho restaurant Bob Bob Ricard. Every table has a 'Press for Champagne' button! Wherever I am going I always plan my wardrobe, try a new lipstick and take time to pamper myself, which makes the evening out more of an occasion. Being surrounded by my friends, eating well, singing, dancing and toasting the season together makes me very happy. Get out there and have loads of fun.

Staying In

I know I have just told you all the brilliant reasons for getting out and about during December and boosting your scores on the elf-o-meter. So what I am about to say next may sound like the opposite, but in fact they go hand in hand: I find that as much as I enjoy going out I also need to plan quiet time for myself. I truly love being at home, with Jim and with friends, but also having time on my own makes me happy.

I am a massive believer in no-makeup days. I like to give my skin the opportunity to breathe and have one less thing to do in the morning. I also regularly schedule in a pamper session at home, whether that is just soaking in a big candlelit *Lush*-scented bubble bath or using a body scrub, putting on a face mask and giving my hair a deep conditioning treatment. In the winter I find my skin can be very dry so I am strict

Top Ten Films

Love Actually

Home Alone

Harry Potter & The Philosopher's Stone

Elf

The Holiday

Miracle on 34th Street

The Muppet Christmas Carol

The Polar Express

Arthur Christmas

The Grinch

about my skincare regime and an obsessive full body moisturiser! I have shared my tried and tested DIY Orange and Ginger Body Scrub (page 92) for you to make your own pamper treat.

One year I got given some super-soft cashmere socks from *The White Company* and now I can't live without them. I have included them in my definitive gift guide later in the book (pages 80–3) as now I know how fab they are I want everyone to have a pair. On a night in I pull these on, get into my pyjamas and head straight to the sofa to snuggle into a pile of cushions and blankets. Sometimes Jim joins me and we chill out together in front of a box-set or one of our Top Ten Christmas films (page 23). My pup Martha is often curled up at my feet, on my lap or she even tries to lie across my head!

However, early nights are crucial and I love to head to bed with a book. Escaping into a literary world is one of the best ways to relax and I have been a bookworm from the moment I learnt to read. I always choose something that enhances my festive mood and have included my Top Ten books for inspiration (page 231).

Down-time at home also gives you the chance to do some Christmas prep. I am never more content than when I am in the kitchen, trying out new recipes, baking batches of cookies and getting organised for the main feast days. This year I am going to make my traditional Christmas Cake in advance. In this chapter I have included my foolproof recipe (page 36) and, later in the book, I have devoted an entire chapter to my cakes, puddings and bakes. That shows my dedication and my sweet tooth!

Often, one or two of my friends will come and join my baking evening. It is so much fun to hang out in the kitchen together and cook. We make treats that can be given as gifts, like Florentines (page 86) and also spend time crafting – making Christmas cards is a good group activity (page 38).

Don't be swayed by all those social media posts that show friends having a fun time while you have chosen to stay at home. You cannot be invited to or go to everything, so be thankful for what you have chosen to do. Relish the time at home and the time on your own because that re-energises you for the days ahead.

Your Christmas Traditions

I am so lucky to be part of such a great social media community. I love to hear about other people's lives so I knew just who to ask when I was looking for Christmas traditions and stories to share. These are some of my favourites, but it was hard to pick! Thank you to all of you who responded, and I am only sorry we couldn't include everyone who replied.

@vna_5
Our family tradition is to go down to the beach with the fam and throw some snags on the barbie!

@sunflowersoul
We go to a neighbourhood that has an endless amount of lights and wear robes and pyjamas and drink hot chocolate.

@Kellzzies
Making stollen with my mum and sister and it turning out different every single time. Putting obnoxious Christmas hats on my parents' cats?

@oliviacrhodes_
We have a Christmas 'yearbook' that all my family write in about their year and what we've done that Christmas with a photo of all of us taken on Christmas Day – it's been going since I was about 5 and it's so fun each year to look back at all the milestones and achievements different members of the family reached in different years!

@BartelsJantje
In Germany we watch a Christmas film on 23rd December and decorate our Christmas tree. On the 24th we prepare Kartoffelsalat (potato salad) together and spend the afternoon at church leading the children's choir and singing in the adult choir. After the services we exchange presents, eat together and open presents. Having a vicar as a father means that Christmas is stressful but it's also one of the merriest times of the year xxx

@Jade_Copper_123
Every year my grandma makes me and my cousins a massive Christmas cracker with lots of little presents in!

@EmmaBines
Our tradition is all getting in cosy PJs, making a hot chocolate and watching The Polar Express. *We only watch it once a year.*

@kimsurratt
The kids in our family perform a variety show. Singing, karaoke, dance numbers, jokes etc. Toddlers to college age.

@grace_chst
We sprinkle oats and glitter – 'reindeer food' – for the reindeers outside our house on Christmas Eve!

@SophieHughen
Our grandma's tradition is called the swan, a little model of a swan filled with choc and given out on Christmas Eve with a little gift.

@FreyaHinsley
We always have Christmas dinner on Christmas Eve so we don't have to spend all of Christmas Day cooking!

@ElenaIsabelle_
My grandad and I always go into the woods and decorate a tree for all the animals so they can celebrate too. We use carrots, nuts, apples and bring bird seeds and we use the same tree every year. It's beautiful and despite me being 4 when we started, I'm still doing it at 23. Decorating a tree for the wildlife became our special tradition and I love it.

@Adunbeex
We get a white Christmas bauble and write everything we've done this year and hang it on the tree.

@Pe_taOnline
My family opens a present an hour on Christmas Day! It goes on all day.

@Charlottehugh1
My grandma made a snowman full of little gifts each with a raffle ticket on. We'd take it in turns to pick a ticket and find the matching gift. You could then swap at the end. It gets quite fun and very competitive!

@bigbirdbazza
We make homemade crackers to open on New Year's Day which is the final present of the holidays and first present of the new year.

@beckamillar
We have a present in a sleigh that we open during our meal – it was a tradition started by my grandad 40 years ago and we still do it!

@katiemansii
When taking our tree down my husband and I write one wish for ourselves and one for each other and put it in the box and open the next Christmas.

@Mol9208
My nan plays the fishing game with us when we see her at Xmas. Lots of gifts wrapped up & a wooden rod to take turns and fish them out!

@jessash7
On Xmas Eve me and my boyfriend always make shortbread men and personalise them for the different family members we see on Christmas Day.

@MrsAtoB_
Mum and I go through the Xmas Radio Times with a highlighter and plan our Xmas TV!

Making Time For Others

We all know Christmas is a time for giving as well as receiving. It's one of the attributes of the season that I enjoy so much and it sums up the true spirit of Christmas. Dr. Seuss wrote, 'Maybe Christmas,' he thought, '*doesn't* come from a store? Maybe Christmas... perhaps... means a little bit more?' in *How The Grinch Stole Christmas*. It's good to be reminded of this in the midst of the prep and panic of December.

One year I went to a beautiful carol concert organised by Crisis at Christmas at London's Southwark Cathedral. There were five speakers, each explaining how the charity had helped them get back on track. It was incredibly moving and poignant and highlighted how important it is to support where you can. There are many excellent organisations who can help you help others in small ways (and much bigger), depending on what you can offer.

- Volunteer – Crisis at Christmas, part of Crisis, the national charity for homelessness, and Shelter need additional support in December. Crisis needs 11,000 volunteers across their nationwide centres. Volunteers must be aged 16 or over, but if you are 16 or 17 you will need a parent or guardian to attend with you.

- Food Banks – A brilliant way to give food directly to those needing it. Get in touch with The Trussell Trust to find out how you can donate or help in your local area.

- Charity Shops – Barnardos, British Heart Foundation and many more charities make an annual appeal for unwanted Christmas presents. Have a look in your cupboards and see if there is anything you received last year that you have never used, and take it along to your local charity shop.

- Donate a winter coat – This is such a great idea. Find a winter coat you no longer wear and give it one of the many charities who are asking for exactly this. Like Wrap Up London, where you can go to one of their London Underground drop-offs, or Unicef, who organise regular parcel deliveries to refugees.

- Christmas Cards – buying Christmas cards can instantly benefit a charity and most have their own beautiful designs for sale in high streets across the country. Or go online and purchase cards directly from charities like the Make A Wish Foundation, who help magical dreams come true for seriously ill children. Once Christmas is over you can take all your cards to participating local supermarkets to be recycled by The Woodland Trust. It's so much better than just throwing them away.

It's good to look closer to home too – I try to keep an eye on those around me and think of a random act of kindness that may make them smile, like taking over some freshly baked cookies to a friend who is feeling a bit down, putting the kettle on and having a catch up. Or helping my mum with some of her present shoppping or wrapping. Little things mean a lot.

Luxury Hazelnut Hot Chocolate

Makes 1 big mugful
Cooking time: 5–10 minutes

300ml milk
2 tbsp hazelnut chocolate
  spread
1 tbsp cocoa powder
squirty cream

To decorate:
a *Flake*, chopped nuts and
marshmallows, to serve
(optional)

How do you like yours? In your favourite mug with a swirl of chocolate spread or a dollop of cream? A scattering of marshmallows or a dash of Irish cream liqueur? You could even set up a hot chocolate station with toppings already prepared for your friends to customise their own.

Gently heat the milk in a small saucepan. As it warms up, whisk in the hazelnut chocolate spread and cocoa powder until smooth and lump free. Once the milk is nice and hot and just beginning to bubble round the edges, remove from the heat and pour into your favourite mug. Top with squirty cream, a *Flake*, some chopped nuts and marshmallows, if you like.

DIY Advent Calendars

You will need:

stiff card (10 x 5cm)

4 sheets of red felt
(22cm square)

4 sheets of green felt
(22cm square)

pins

sharp scissors

embroidery thread –
1 skein red/1 skein
green

embroidery needle

PVA glue

red ribbon or string
(to hang your
stockings from)

penny sweets

Every year when I was young my mum hung up an adorable mini felt stocking advent calendar on our mantelpiece and filled it with sweets. This was the moment that signalled the beginning of December and took festive anticipation to new levels! I have created a homemade version – an exact replica of what I had as a child – as I couldn't buy it anywhere and I wanted it just like it used to be (because I am sentimental like that). You could stuff yours with chocolate, tiny gifts or little mottos. If you use sweets, make sure they are wrapped – if they're not, they'll become sticky in the lead up to Christmas Day.

❅ Draw and cut out a stocking shape (about 5cm wide by 10cm tall) from a piece of card. Use this template to draw around and cut out 24 green and 24 red shapes from the felt (draw on the back of the felt to hide the pen marks).

❅ Take one red and one green stocking and choose which will be the front and the back. Pin together and use sharp scissors to trim around the edge so they match exactly.

❅ Cut a length of embroidery thread, about 50cm long. Carefully pull apart the thread, so you have two lengths of 3 strands each. Thread one length (all 3 strands) into your needle and use blanket stitch or running stitch all around the edge of the stocking, leaving the top open. Sew the rest of the stockings together, using more thread when necessary, remembering to

do half with red fronts and half with green and making sure they all face the right direction.

❅ Cut out 12 strips of green felt 1cm wide that will fit around the top of your stockings. Cut out 12 matching ones in red. Use running stitch and matching thread to sew contrasting coloured felt around the top of each stocking.

❅ Cut out 12 tabs of felt (4 x 1cm) in green felt and 12 matching ones in red. Fold the tabs in half and stitch to the top front edge of each stocking, matching the front colour.

❅ Lay out the stockings in alternate colours. Cut out numbers 1 to 24 in contrasting colours and stick them to the stockings with dots of glue.

❅ Hang your stockings evenly along the ribbon or string and fill each with a sweet, or several!

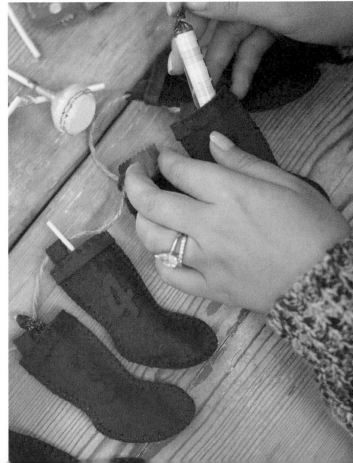

Christmas Cake

Serves 12–16
Prep time: 45 minutes
Cooking time: 2 hours

200g sultanas
200g raisins
200g dates, chopped
200g dried figs, chopped
100g dried cranberries
100g currants
grated zest and juice of
    2 oranges
grated zest and juice of
    1 lemon
50ml brandy, plus extra to
    feed your cake after
    cooking
250g butter, in pieces
200g soft light brown sugar
175g plain flour
½ tsp baking powder
2 tsp mixed spice
1 tsp ground cinnamon
½ tsp ground ginger
100g ground almonds
100g flaked almonds
4 large eggs
1 tsp vanilla extract
1 tbsp treacle

To decorate:
icing sugar, for dusting
800g golden marzipan
3 tbsp apricot jam, warmed
800g white icing, ready
    to roll

*You will need a 20cm
loose-bottomed cake tin.*

I know it's not everyone's favourite cake, but I've perfected a seriously delicious recipe and Christmas just isn't the same without it. Traditionally, it should be made several months in advance, fed with brandy every fortnight and decorated a day or so before you plan to eat it. It makes the most stunning centrepiece, with a winter wonderland on top, but if it really isn't your thing, try my white Christmas cake, on page 164.

Mix the dried fruit, zests and juice, brandy, butter and sugar in a large saucepan. Bring to the boil over a medium-high heat, then turn the heat to low and simmer for 5–10 minutes. Remove from the heat and, after a few minutes, tip into a large mixing bowl to cool for 25 minutes.

Preheat the oven to 150°C/300°F/gas mark 2. Line the cake tin with a double layer of baking parchment, letting it come up about 7.5cm higher than the sides of the tin.

Add the dry ingredients, spices and nuts to the fruit mixture and stir to combine. Lightly beat the eggs, then stir in the vanilla and treacle. Add to the fruit, and stir gently to combine. Tip into the prepared tin and level the top with a spatula. Bake in the centre of the oven for 2 hours. Take the cake out of the oven, poke holes in it with a skewer and spoon over 2 tablespoons of brandy. Leave to cool completely in the tin.

Once cool, peel off the baking parchment and wrap in clingfilm. Feed the cake every 2 weeks by unwrapping and drizzling with 1–2 tablespoons of brandy. Don't feed it in the week before Christmas so it can dry out a little.

Dust your work surface with icing sugar and roll the marzipan out to a thickness of about 1cm, and to a circle about 5cm bigger than your cake. Flip your cake upside down, and brush the sides and the flat top with warm jam. Lift the marzipan over the cake and smooth it over and around the cake. Trim any excess from around the base of the cake.

Roll out the icing on a work surface dusted with icing sugar to about 5mm thick. Lift the icing over the cake, and smooth down the top and sides, pressing out any air bubbles. Trim any excess from around the base and place on a plate or cake stand. Wrap with a wide ribbon and decorate the top with a Christmassy scene.

Christmas Cards

You will need:

large rubber stamp that
will fit on your card
(The English Stamp
Company are great!)
ink pad or pads in
different colours
packs of plain cards with
envelopes
PVA glue
paintbrush
glitter pots
newspaper (to protect
your work surface!)

Making your own Christmas cards is such a lovely, personal craft and one that all your family and friends can enjoy the benefit of. I prefer brown cards but any colour looks lovely with the right stamped inks. It's totally up to you what stamps you use, and nothing says Christmas like a generous dusting of glitter, so feel free to add it to bring out some of the detail.

* Take the stamp of your choice and press it into the ink pad, making sure it is evenly coloured with ink. It's a good idea to test the stamp on some scrap paper so you get used to using it.

* Stamp it firmly and evenly on to the front cover of your card. Lift off the stamp and leave to dry.

* I would actually suggest writing your cards at this point as adding the glitter can make them a bit messy.

* Once all your cards are stamped and written, lay them all out on newspaper.

* Use the paintbrush to add little spots of glue or edge the image with glue – wherever you would like the glitter to settle – but only use light dots of glue!

* Shake the glitter liberally over the glue on the card.

* Shake off the excess glitter onto the newspaper and repeat with the remaining cards.

A Night With The Girls

I have amazing friends, and some of them I've known since school days. Over the years, no matter what we are doing or where we are, we make time for each other. During the first week of December I cook dinner for my old school gang: Kate, Maddie, Emma and Vanessa. We toast the yuletide with prosecco, eat dinner, laugh, gossip and always end up dancing on our chairs! Every year we have a picture taken of us all under the tree, swap Secret Santa gifts, and the evening ends in a giant sleepover. Followed by a massive cooked breakfast the following morning!

If you are inspired by this, whether it's arranging a big dinner, having a few friends over for a drink or a more practical crafting evening, remember my basics for setting the scene: get your Christmas playlist on, fairy lights and candles at the ready and make your dining table festive. Don't forget those little touches like Christmas crackers, too. If you can, plan your menu and shop the day before the event (although I am hopeless at this and enjoy a last-minute dash around the supermarket). Once your guests have arrived, offer them a drink or get everyone in the party mood instantly by encouraging them to make their own cocktails. I have included my all-time favourites on pages 122–5.

Feeding my friends is at the heart of my love for baking and cooking and I like to try out new recipes on them. Many of the dishes that I have included in this book have been shared and enjoyed around my dining table. One memorable dinner started with my crowd-pleasing Baked Camembert 3 Ways (page 44) and was followed by a Turkey, Leek and Mushroom Pie (page 232). Pudding depends entirely on what I fancy at the time, but is often something indulgent, like a rich chocolate mousse (page 170), trifle (page 172) or cheesecake (page 174).

We always organise a Secret Santa between the five of us, although it doesn't stay secret for long. In the past, Jim has popped on a Santa hat and handed the gifts out but that is the only part he is allowed to join us for. It is girls' night after all! Do remember that although you are the host you need to enjoy your evening too, so don't attempt anything that takes you out of your comfort zone.

There are lots of other ways to entertain your friends without the formality or pressure of a sit-down dinner. It may just be a couple of you who want to get together and make the evening a cooking or crafting session. My friend Scarlett and I love nothing more than a big baking afternoon. It's a great way to tackle homemade gifts like batch-cooking trays of biscotti, chopping mountains of vegetables for chutney or even just wrapping your presents together. Tackling these delightful festive chores is undoubtedly more fun with company and means you achieve more, too.

I don't think I will ever grow out of sleepovers. Zoe and I love to go to each other's houses, get a big tin of Christmas chocolates and watch a film. We have a tradition of buying each other Christmas pyjamas every year and they usually have robins on! The brilliant thing about sleepovers is that you still have the morning together to go out for a big breakfast.

DIY Place Names

You will need:

foliage – a couple of
    sprigs of rosemary,
    conifer, ivy or bay,
    or a mixture, for
    each table setting
brown string
brown labels
white pen

I love these foliage place names. They are little bouquets of Christmassy greenery and you can include anything you may have to hand. Herbs like rosemary work well but also fir tree sprigs and ivy. You can tie in a little decoration like a star and add your label with the name written on. Alternatively, you can tie them round napkins like napkin rings. They add greenery to a table if you are tight on space for a centrepiece arrangement.

❄ Create small bunches of greenery using a couple of sprigs of foliage (approx. 7cm long). I find for shape and smell rosemary, conifer, ivy or bay work very well. You want to make button-hole-sized bunches, one for each place setting. Secure each bundle at the base with brown string.

❄ Use a parcel label as a place name. Write your guests' names with white pen and tie it to the bunch with a fresh piece of string.

❄ Give it a little tweak so the name label is visible.

Starter
Crostini three ways

Entrée
Fish pie with cheddar mash

Dessert
Sticky toffee & pear traybake

Drinks
Clementine & cranberry bellini
Pomegranate fizz

Tanya ⚝

Baked Camembert 3 Ways

Each baked cheese serves
 6–8
Prep time for each:
 5 minutes
Cooking time for each:
 15–25 minutes

The first time I baked a camembert I didn't realise it had to stay in its box and I popped it in the oven directly on the shelf. My friend Vanessa and I watched through the oven door excitedly, only to see melting cheese dripping through the rack.
We couldn't stop laughing and I have never made the same mistake again. All three of these versions are equal winners at my Girls' Night In. Serve the baked cheese with some crudités, sliced baguette or ciabatta, breadsticks and crackers, if you like.

1 whole camembert,
 with its wooden box
3 tbsp cranberry sauce,
 homemade (see recipe
 on page 213) or from a jar

CAMEMBERT TOPPED WITH CRANBERRY SAUCE

Preheat the oven to 200°C/400°F/gas mark 6.

Remove the camembert from its box and remove any paper or plastic wrapping. Place it back in the bottom half of its box and pierce the top of the cheese several times with a knife, not going all the way through.

Spoon the cranberry sauce over top and cover the cheese very loosely with foil.

Place the cheese in its box on a baking tray and bake it in the oven for 12 minutes, then remove the foil and pop it back in the oven for 3–5 minutes or until the cheese has melted and the cranberry sauce is bubbly and hot. Serve hot.

1 whole camembert, with its
 wooden box
2 garlic cloves, very thinly
 sliced
leaves stripped from
 1 big sprig of rosemary
1 tbsp olive oil

CAMEMBERT STUDDED WITH ROSEMARY AND GARLIC

Preheat the oven to 200°C/400°F/gas mark 6.

Remove the camembert from its box and remove any paper or plastic wrapping. Place it back in the bottom half of its box and pierce the top of the cheese several times with a knife, not going all the way through.

Carefully wedge some garlic slices and rosemary leaves into each hole on top of the cheese, pressing them in with your fingertips. Drizzle the olive oil over the top.

Place the cheese in its box on a baking tray and bake it in the oven for 15–20 minutes or until the cheese has melted. Serve hot.

1 ready-rolled sheet of puff
   pastry (320g)
plain flour, for dusting
1 whole camembert
1 egg, beaten

CAMEMBERT WRAPPED IN PUFF PASTRY WITH A BOW

Take the sheet of pastry out of the fridge 20 minutes before you start cooking, and preheat the oven to 200°C/400°F/gas mark 6. Line a baking sheet with baking parchment.

Dust the work surface with flour and lay the sheet of pastry on top. Cut out two circles of pastry that are 2cm larger than the cheese (you can use the lid of the box as a template). Also cut out two long 2cm-wide strips.

Remove the camembert from its box and remove any paper or plastic wrapping. Place the cheese on one of the rounds, and tuck the edges of pastry up the sides of the cheese. Place the second circle of pastry on top of the cheese and tuck the top edges down around the sides. Seal and brush with some beaten egg.

Wrap one of the long pastry strips around the cheese and seal the edge with some more beaten egg. Make your second strip of pastry into a bow and place it on top. Brush the whole thing with egg and pop it on the lined baking sheet.

Pop the pastry-wrapped cheese in the oven for 25 minutes, or until the pastry is puffed up and golden brown. Serve hot.

S'Mores

Makes 10
Prep time: 15 minutes
Cooking time: 5 minutes

20 biscuits made using the
Melting Snowman
Cookies recipe on page
152, baked in festive
shapes if you like, or
digestive biscuits, if
you prefer
10 squares milk or dark
chocolate
10 large marshmallows

*You will need some fireproof
skewers.*

These bring back memories of my first home with Jim, where we had an open fire. On cold wintry afternoons we would make s'mores as a treat. Now we live in London and make these over the fire pit. You can even grill them! There is nothing finer or more Christmassy than being with your friends, toasting marshmallows and sandwiching them between biscuits with squares of chocolate.

Lay half your biscuits out on a plate or tray and top each one with a piece of chocolate.

Spear a marshmallow onto a metal skewer and hold it over an open flame. Keep turning them until the marshmallow softens and begins to brown. Use a fork to slide the marshmallow off the skewer onto the chocolate-topped biscuit and sandwich with a second biscuit. Devour immediately! Repeat with the remaining marshmallows.

If you've not got an open flame or fire, you can make these under a medium–high grill by topping a biscuit with a piece of chocolate, then the marshmallow and popping the stack under the preheated grill for 4–5 minutes, or until the marshmallow begins to brown and melt. Be sure to keep your eye on them because they can burn very easily. Remove from the grill and top with a second biscuit.

Mulled Wine

Serves 4
Prep time: 3 minutes
Cooking time: 15 minutes

1 x 750ml bottle red wine
100g caster sugar
3 cloves
1 cinnamon stick
1 bay leaf
½ tsp freshly grated nutmeg
3 clementines, (skin on)
    sliced, plus extra to
    decorate

To decorate:
thinly sliced apple
cinnamon sticks

It makes the house smell amazing, my friends love it, you can keep topping it up and the process of putting it together makes me feel instantly festive. It's the drink equivalent of listening to a Michael Bublé Christmas album!

Add all the ingredients to a saucepan, and heat gently over a medium-low heat, stirring occasionally until the sugar is dissolved. Leave to infuse gently for about 10 minutes, but don't allow it to simmer or boil.

Ladle into heatproof glasses or cups, and serve with thinly sliced apple, clementine slices and cinnamon sticks.

CHAPTER TWO
Deck the Halls

Deck the Halls

There is nothing more heart-warming than coming home at the end of a busy December day to a house filled with fairy lights and the Christmassy scents of clove and cinnamon. I truly believe that creating a space you love can increase your quality of life on lots of levels. I absolutely know that when my home is the way I like it I feel calmer and able to focus. The same goes for decorating the house at Christmas – it puts me instantly in the mood to celebrate!

Home may be with your parents, or in a flat-share with friends, or you may have your own place. Whatever space is yours to decorate, there are always opportunities to create your very own Santa's grotto atmosphere and I have loads of ideas to help you out. A mad dash around the house on Christmas Eve with strings of lights, baubles and holly is just not fun. I give myself a day in early December to unpack boxes of lights and decorations, put the tree up and garland the bannisters, all to the backdrop of carols playing and mince pies baking.

Don't be overwhelmed by the mass of Christmas decorations that start to go on sale from the end of the summer. It's brilliant to pop into the big department stores when their displays are out, to get some inspiration, but don't feel compelled to buy. Selfridges and Harrods have entire floors dedicated to decorations and Liberty is famous for its Christmas emporium. I can't resist a visit to The White Company

for their scented candles and pot pourri, but you don't have to spend much money. In this chapter I will show you how you can also make things like this yourself and enjoy the satisfaction of hanging homemade decorations on your tree.

The Christmas tree is undoubtedly the central point of decking the halls. From choosing, positioning and deciding on a theme (or joyfully covering it with everything!) this is the decoration around which your Christmas unfolds. I know other families put their presents under the tree as they wrap them or are given them, and this growing pile looks instantly festive, but our presents don't appear under the tree until Santa has been… this is just the way we have always done it!

I am a big fan of interiors magazines, books and websites and am constantly inspired by them for my own home. In this chapter I also include some of the images that I refer to for my own surroundings, from minimalism to old-fashioned crimson and gold opulence. I am in heaven looking through photos of glistening snow scenes, cosy sofas by roaring fires and sparkling fairy lights crammed everywhere! I find it almost impossible to decide which theme to go with as I love it all.

Going up into the attic to find last year's decorations is always an exciting moment and unwrapping family favourites and things you have made as a child instantly brings back memories of Christmases past. Dad really goes for it every year with his Christmas lights display and flashing reindeer at the front of the house! I think it's important to add a new decoration each year too, something that will help your collection grow and be an instant reminder in future years of a place or time.

However you choose to decorate, the rule is there are no rules. Make your Christmas glitzy, dazzling and beautiful in any way you want it, but remember that whatever you do will need a little planning and enough time to pull it off. And there is always a place for tinsel.

Creating a Festive Atmosphere

I love creating the right atmosphere and I really appreciate going to other people's houses where they do the same. There are key elements for me that I think need to be considered, no matter what the space limitations.

Most importantly, you want to be comfortable and relaxed in your home and you want your family and friends to feel the same the instant they walk through the door. The first step is to give everywhere a good old-fashioned clean and hoover before you begin to think about decorations. Stray cobwebs may work at Halloween but they aren't welcome at Christmas. I love doing this because often it makes me have a huge clear-out which is always a good thing.

Think about how you want the room or the house to smell – this is central to building a good ambience and can immediately conjure festive memories. I focus on all the iconic yuletide scents like orange, cinnamon, clove and pine needles and repeat them in various ways using candles, pot pourri (I always put a large bowl in the empty

fireplace of my bedroom), essential oils, maybe a discreet diffuser, but also putting the scents in my baking and decoration making. A simmering pan of mulled wine on the stove fills the entire house with its enticing aroma. As does a batch of gingerbread muffins fresh from the oven. The tree gives off the clean, sharp smell of pine, which is one of the reasons why I choose a real one.

Good lighting is essential to interiors generally, but comes into its own at Christmas. Keep the lighting low, glowing and warm, with lots of lamps and twinkly lights. I am literally obsessed by fairy lights and I use them outside (solar) and inside (battery operated) around bannisters, headboards, plants and coiled in glass jars.

A vase of white cut flowers and hyacinth bulbs in a pot by your bed or on the dining-room table is a stylishly simple way of bringing the outside in. If you live in the country you could collect greenery like holly and ivy from a wintry walk and create a wreath, garland or table display. Alternatively, drape ivy over picture frames – often this is all you need to make a room look instantly more festive. I always have a massive bunch of mistletoe hanging in the house as I think it looks beautiful for decoration, and there's the tradition of a kiss underneath it!

Once you have covered all these basics, take a look at the Christmas decorations you already have and think about what theme you might like. This could be inspired by a shop display, blog, traditional Christmases or a new set of decorations. You may want to mix it up and fill every spare space with a festive flourish. Remember all the Christmas cards you will be receiving and think about how you might want to display them: it looks really effective to attach the cards to lengths of ribbon using mini pegs (Paperchase always stocks them) and hanging them horizontally from the bannister. Or put up a string washing line in the kitchen and peg the cards on to that. Jim and I still do stockings for each other and always hang them by the fireplace as a decoration before taking them to my parents' house to lay on the end of our bed on Christmas Eve.

Swapping everyday items for a festive version is an instant mood lifter. My December morning cup of tea is always in one of my Christmas mugs (my favourite is the reindeer one) and starts the day as I mean to go on. I have a cupboard in the kitchen full of themed crockery and kitchen accessories like my snowman-shaped biscuit cutters and Christmas tree-shaped chopping board. I will admit I am also quite child-like with our bedding as it is only for one month of the year. It's something I have some real fun with and don't mind if it isn't my usual style. Asda and M&S do some amazing Christmas bedding and my favourite is the brushed cotton because it is so cosy for this time of year.

It really is possible to add that special magic to whatever space and budget you have to work with, so get decorating!

I love creating little corners of Christmas all over the house (and garden) so wherever I look I can see some festive cheer. Here are some of my favourite ways to decorate, and some inspirational photos:

❄ A roaring open fire instantly transports me to cosy, Christmassy times and marshmallow toasting. Not only that but a decorated mantelpiece makes the perfect festive focal point to the room and is where we hang our stockings before Christmas Eve.

❄ I think bedrooms should have the same festive love as the rest of the house. Entwining fairy lights, making the bed up with Christmas linen and lighting a winter scented candle creates a magical sanctuary.

❄ How lovely to greet your Christmas guests with a warm and inviting hallway. Good lighting, somewhere to hang coats and leave bags, a bowl of pot pourri and a massive bunch of mistletoe is a great start.

❄ You can never have too many candles at Christmas. I love candlelit evenings and the instant glowing atmosphere they create. Use them wherever you can safely, or replace them with jars of fairy lights.

❄ Bringing greenery into the house is such a beautiful, cheap and easy way to decorate, or fake it with realistic garlands. I like to make a statement with my bannisters by wrapping foliage and fairy lights around them and hanging mini decorations.

❄ Don't limit your baubles to the Christmas tree. Hang them in front of windows, fill bowls with them and add them to any decorative arrangements.

❄ Creating a cosy, festive nook in your garden with outside fairy lights makes the ideal spot to drink hot chocolate, watch the stars and add another log to the fire pit.

Christmas Tree, Oh Christmas Tree

The Christmas tree is the majestic centrepiece of our entire celebration and I couldn't imagine December without it. I know it is very early for some, but getting the tree is the first thing I do in the month. Once I get to the 1st December it's all I can think about, and every part from the choosing, buying, bringing it home and decorating makes me so happy.

We didn't have a real tree when I was growing up but we did visit Notcutts in Norwich to get in the mood and choose a couple of decorations. Now I have my own house I get my tree from Petersham Nurseries in Richmond and plan a lunch trip around it. Buying early in the month means you are better off getting a Nordman Fir, as they last longer, but if the tree will only be up for a couple of weeks then a Norway Spruce is good. If you can buy from a local grower then do, but otherwise they are available from supermarkets, DIY stores, farm shops and reputable market stalls.

Make sure you have an idea of the measurements for where you want it to go, and see the tree fully displayed from all angles before you buy it. The first home Jim and I shared was a barn conversion with a vaulted ceiling. I thought it would be fabulous to get a massive tree to suit the ten-foot space, so we did. Instead, what happened was that we ended up nearly falling off the ladder because that was the only way we

could decorate it. It was dangerous just trying to string the fairy lights around it! Safe to say, a seven-foot tree is now my limit. Don't be afraid to give your tree a little pruning to make it fit the space – you can always lop a bit off the top or take off a couple of branches. Putting it in a proper tree stand with water will make it last twice as long and encourage the needles not to fall.

My tree takes pride of place in the bay window of the sitting room so I can look at it as often as possible. It's a good spot in my house but you may prefer yours in a hallway or dining room. Just remember, you need to be near a socket for all those fairy lights. Getting two trees can be the answer if you can't decide where to put them, or you want to use different decorating themes. It is such a cute idea to have a mini tree in your bedroom with tiny battery-operated lights and small baubles. There are excellent fake tree alternatives, or you could go obviously artificial with shimmering silver tinsel boughs (no dropped needles to worry about there).

Decorating your tree is all a matter of personal taste. Always start by putting the lights on and making sure they are evenly distributed. If you packed your decorations away carefully from the year before there shouldn't be any breakages, but check through and decide which you will use. I am a big fan of the snowy, glittery gold look. Alternatively, I could easily embrace the traditional style with theatrical reds and greens. Think about a decoration you are drawn to like the nutcracker soldier, a jolly Santa, candy canes or something homemade, and use that as a starting point. My Stained Glass Edible Decorations (page 66) look so beautiful hanging from the tree or in front of a window. Tinsel is out of favour but don't let that stop you if you can't imagine your tree without it.

When you are happy with the overall effect of your tree, it is time for the crowning glory – the star or the angel on top. Jim and I always have a star. Stand back, countdown '3,2,1', switch on the fairy lights and admire. Ta-dah!

Make Your Own Wreath

You will need:

35cm diameter copper
or wire wreath frame
8 generous handfuls of
moss (foraged or
from a florist)
floristry wire
garden string
armfuls of foliage e.g.
conifer, ivy,
eucalyptus, bay,
mistletoe
decorative items e.g.
pine cones, berries,
twigs, cinnamon
sticks, dried orange
slices (page 68),
ribbons

I learnt to make a Christmas wreath at Petersham Nurseries, and it was one of the best ways to spend a December day. Creating a show-stopping decoration for your house or to give as a gift is such a feeling of achievement. It is also brilliant to learn a new skill that can then be put to good use every year. Making a wreath is not difficult, it just requires the right kit, a good selection of greenery and some patience. If you make only one thing I would encourage you to do this and, even better, organise for friends to come over so you can make them together.

❋ Pad out the wreath frame with moss, ensuring there are no gaps. Wrap wire or tightly wind garden string around the moss to hold it in place and create a compact base.

❋ Either create small sprigs of mixed foliage, tie them, then attach them to your base with wire for a more uniform look, or poke individual pieces onto your wreath. If doing the latter, make sure the stems push through the moss and stay in place then secure where you need to with wire or string. As you attach the greenery, remember to do it in the same direction so you can overlap them slightly.

❋ Step back and look at your wreath, or ask someone to hold it up for you. This is the best way to check if there are any gaps and that it is evenly arranged.

❋ The final decorations bring the whole thing together. You can use pine cones, dried orange slices, berries, cinnamon sticks and decorations. It is tempting to overload the wreath but bear in mind how heavy it will be and the door you will be displaying it on.

❋ Hold your wreath up and decide where you want the top to be. You can tie a festive ribbon round the wreath at this point, tucking it in behind the greenery and using the ends to hang it from. Or you can hang the wreath directly on a nail.

Stained Glass Edible Decorations

Makes about 30
Prep time: 15 minutes
Cooking time: 12 minutes

75g unsalted butter,
    softened
75g dark muscovado sugar
1 egg
1½ tbsp golden syrup
200g plain flour, plus extra
    for dusting
½ tsp baking powder
1 tsp ground cinnamon
¼ tsp freshly grated nutmeg
¼ tsp ground ginger
30 clear boiled sweets,
    removed from any
    wrapping

You will need Christmas cookie cutters as well as simple, smaller cookie cutter shapes (like hearts, circles or stars) and ribbon or string.

It's always fun to have something edible hanging from your tree. Here I have elevated the humble cookie decoration to a glowing stained glass biscuit. They look so beautiful dangling from the branches with fairy lights glinting through them or hanging in your window. You can choose a whole host of cutter shapes – I couldn't resist these baubles – and play around with sweet colours or further embellish the biscuit with icing, if you fancy. These also work really well as a gift that may never make it to the tree…

Preheat the oven to 180°C/350°F/gas mark 4. Line 2 baking trays with baking parchment.

Put the butter and sugar in a bowl and beat together until light and fluffy. Add the egg and golden syrup and combine well, then mix in the flour, baking powder and spices to make a smooth dough.

Dust the work surface with flour. Tip the mixture out onto the surface and roll it out to a thickness of 3–4mm. Cut out some large shapes with Christmas cookie cutters, transfer these shapes onto your baking trays, then cut out some smaller shapes from the inside of the bigger ones, to create space for your stained-glass effect. You can re-roll the dough that you've removed from the centres to make more cookies until you've used up all the dough (you should end up with about 30 biscuits). Using a straw, poke out a hole at the top of each biscuit.

Bake the biscuits in the oven for 5 minutes, then remove from the oven. Place a boiled sweet into each shape you've cut from the centre of the decorations. If the shapes you've cut won't fit a whole sweet, crush the sweet into chunks in a mortar and pestle (or with a rolling pin) and add the broken bits. You can mix colours by breaking the sweets into pieces and adding a few pieces of different coloured sweets to each hole. If the hole for the ribbon looks like it has closed over, carefully open it again with a skewer.

Return the biscuits to the oven for 6 minutes, or just until the sweets have melted to fill the shapes. Remove from the oven and leave to cool completely on the baking trays before carefully looping lengths of ribbon or string through the holes and hanging them on your tree.

DIY Pot Pourri

You will need:

10 cloves

10 star anise

6 cinnamon sticks

2 handfuls of pine cones
(a mix of sizes)

20 dried orange slices
(see below)

at least 2 of your favourite
festive essential oils,
e.g. orange, cinnamon,
pine and clove

I find the best mix of ingredients that look good and smell great are cinnamon sticks, cloves, pine cones and dried orange slices. You can adapt the mix as you wish, but remember you will be piling it into a big bowl or putting it in a cellophane bag to give as a present. When it comes to the essential oils, I love to echo the clove and orange scent, with maybe a dash of pine for freshness.

❄ Mix all the ingredients together gently in a big bowl and add a few drops of essential oils.

❄ Cover the bowl with a tea towel and leave for a few hours so the essential oils can soak into the pot pourri.

❄ Pop into your display bowl or into gift bags and enjoy the smell of Christmas! Refresh with oil when the scent starts to fade.

Dried Orange Slices

These make such a versatile decoration, on their own or popped into my Pot Pourri. I also love them as Christmas tree decorations. If you do want to use them for the tree, remember to make a little hole in each slice before they go in the oven so you can thread some ribbon through.

❄ To make about 20 slices, slice 3 oranges with a sharp knife into rounds no thicker than 1cm.

❄ Turn your oven on to 100°C/200°F/gas mark ¼ and lay out the slices directly on a rack, putting a tray at the bottom of the oven to catch any juice.

❄ Cook the slices for 4 hours, remembering to turn them every so often, then take out of the oven and leave them in a warm place

overnight. If they are still a little sticky, you can pop them back in the oven for a bit longer or leave them near a radiator to dry out.

❄ The colour will darken so you should be able to see when they are ready to use but touch them to check.

DIY Christmas Scene Tealight Holder

You will need:

glass jam jar
piece of black card long
    enough to wrap
    around your chosen
    jar so the ends meet
template for design
    drawn on contrasting
    paper
craft knife

I am a big fan of candles, so wanted to come up with a craft idea that I could make myself. These give such a glow and create a gorgeous silhouette. It's worth taking the time over cutting the design out because the result is amazing. You could change the design to include your own house or pet, but don't skimp on the windows because they look so effective. I like to make a few and line them up along the mantelpiece, or arrange them with other candles on my Christmas table.

❅ Take your jam jar and wrap the black card around it to make sure it's the right length. It works best if the silhouette comes about halfway up the side of the jar.

❅ Cut out your template and turn it over. Lay it on the reverse of the black card. Draw around it using a pencil.

❅ Use a craft knife to cut out the template, carefully cutting out the windows.

❅ Dot the pencil-marked side with glue and then turn it over and wrap around the base of the jar. Press lightly to fix it to the jar.

❅ Pop a tealight candle in the jar!

CHAPTER THREE
Christmas Gifting

Christmas Gifting

A big part – maybe too big a part – of Christmas is about the pile of presents under the tree. Writing to Father Christmas was one of the most magical moments of the build-up when I was little – I thought hard about what I could ask for and hoped my dreams would come true. The idea that he came swooping through the starry skies with a huge sack of presents precariously perched on the back of his sleigh was amazing! The year I remember most vividly was when I asked for a 'curly bear' that I had been desperate for since seeing him in a shop with Mum and Dad.

I also asked for a HUGE bar of *Cadbury Dairy Milk* – I have always been obsessed with chocolate and I remember going into Woolworths (who remembers Woolworths?!) and seeing one so big I couldn't quite believe it. I wanted it so much that I was so

happy on Christmas morning when I got both. I couldn't believe the size of the chocolate – I must have been pretty small. When I talk about this memory Mum says it was a 500g or 750g bar, but I remember it being almost half the size of me! As I got older, I spent more time thinking about what those around me would love rather than what I wanted myself. Now I am never happier than when I have found the perfect present or thought of the best idea for someone. This doesn't have to be about spending money; it really is the thought that counts. It just takes

time to have that thought and at Christmas, when there are so many other things to do, it is easy to resort to overspending and stress at the very time you don't need it.

Shopping in December can be so much fun. I love wrapping up warmly, meeting friends, going into my favourite store, finding special gifts that I know people will love, stopping off for a delicious lunch and ending the day with a pile of bags at my feet and a cocktail in my hand. It's a mix of exhaustion and achievement! There are also those days where I come home empty-handed after trudging around the shops, jostled by the crowds, unable to find the right present or inspiration, panicking because I am running out of time. Sound familiar?!

In this chapter I am going to take some of the strain out of present buying and have come up with lots of ideas so you don't have to. Let's turn it back into a fun and joyful thing to do, a wonderful way to make family and friends feel extra special. I have tried to cover all bases so there will be something for everyone.

Secret Santa is becoming more popular, not just at work between colleagues but also among families. It is a great way of making Christmas about spending time together rather than having to buy masses of presents, and I've got plenty of ideas for this, too.

We know that presents aren't about the amount of money spent, but the thought you have put into it and knowing what the recipient loves. Nothing says this better than a homemade gift. You get double the joy – firstly in the making of it and secondly when you hand it over! As you know, I don't need an excuse to cook, so a lot of the presents I make are food related and I have chosen a couple to share with you like my Florentines (page 86) and Red Onion Chutney (page 88) here in this chapter. Organising a crafting afternoon with friends is also a brilliant way to make

presents together like my Photo Album (page 90). I have even got something for the pups in our lives, as we could never leave them out, especially since mine thinks she is human!

How To Choose The Perfect Gift

I spend as much time as possible thinking about what everyone would like and hoping that I have got it right. Realistically, I know it isn't always easy to do this for various reasons like cost and practicality, so when I talk about the perfect gift I don't mean something big, expensive and showy. I just mean the right thing for the right person, which is more about thought and effort.

I try to start thinking about Christmas presents as early as I can, and listen out for any ideas or hints that may help. If you are super organised then keep a note somewhere to remind you because it may be months before you start shopping. I hate to get towards December knowing I had the perfect idea for someone and not being able to remember what it was! I also keep an eye out for the gift guides that come up on blogs and in magazines as there are often great suggestions. I have put my own one together in this chapter based on past successes I have had and things I have been given that I have loved.

First things first, write a list. Put down everyone you need to give a present to, from parents, partners, friends and neighbours to the postman and dogs! This way you can see how many people you are buying for and work out an approximate cost of each to give you an idea of budget. Now go through and make a note of those people who you already have ideas for, and add to the list. Finally, go through it again and see how many would prefer something homemade. This gives you a really good starting point.

I try to spot and pick up presents as early as a couple of months before the big day. It's good to spread the cost and means that if you see something, get it, because it may not still be there in December. I also make sure I have a couple of shopping days in the diary where I can head into town and get several gifts in one go, as well as a few hours on the internet. There are always people I am stuck on so I make sure I go to a store I know they love, or a favoured brand, or think about a hobby they may have. If I am still stuck, then heading to the bookshop is a great option, even if it just gives me the excuse to browse for an hour.

No matter how small (or big) your present is, you can immediately make it extra special by how you wrap it. I am a big fan of proper wrapping, using my home-stamped paper, labels, big bows and sometimes even sprigs of foliage. For my ideas on how to make your wrapping extra-personal, carry on reading this chapter. Being given a carefully thought-out gift presented in such a beautiful way is just such a wonderful thing!

To father Christmas

I love you

lapland

I love you

December, 1996

Tanyas Chirstmas list
Walkie talkies
red bows for teddys   ears e cloths for teddy

navy ~~seed~~ coat with gold ~~botto~~ buttons brown
fury bit round the coller

Dear Santa claus

I believe in you
and love you and I
hope you love seeing children.

Love

Tanya

December, 1995

All They Want For Christmas

LOVE AND LUXURY

Nothing says 'I love you' like a classic gift. I am obsessed with pyjamas – novelty ones and monogrammed silk – as well as a cosy dressing gown.

- ❄ Socks are traditionally boring but not when they are luxurious cashmere (try them once and you'll never go back), or opt for thick, woolly and practical welly socks. Maybe a pair of *Hunter* wellies to go with them?

- ❄ A gorgeous knitted jumper is always a big hit in my house. I buy one for Jim every year.

- ❄ Everyone knows a gadget lover and I would recommend a camera – the iconic *Leica*, the fun *Instax Fuji* or the *GoPro*. Alternatively, a bit of kit to go with a camera or an *iPhone*, like the *Olloclip* lens.

- ❄ Personalised stationery is a beautiful thing: a new diary or notebook with the recipient's initials on make it extra special.

- ❄ I know candles are an obvious choice, but if you can push the budget, pick up a *Diptyque* scented candle for unbeatable style and long-lasting smell.

KITCHEN AND HOME

I love receiving gifts for the home, particularly anything connected with the kitchen.

- For the coffee lover in your life, check out the selection of coffee grinders, cafetières and milk steamers. Or buy a bag of freshly ground coffee from your favourite local deli, maybe some jars of preserves, pickles and oils, too.

- The biggest treat, and a brilliant way to say thank you as well as Happy Christmas, is a food hamper – Fortnum and Mason's are renowned for theirs but most food stores do them.

- There is always a new wave of cookbooks out in the autumn so choose a style of food the recipient may not have cooked before.

- Combine fun with practicality and give a cocktail shaker or bottle opener, maybe with a specially distilled gin, a decanter, or a set of martini glasses (*Oliver Bonas* has a great range).

- If you have a committed foodie on your list then a popcorn maker is a good idea, or blow the budget and splash out on a *Kitchen Aid* food mixer.

- A monthly subscription for an interiors, lifestyle or food magazine is the gift that keeps on giving, and the perfect present to post.

- For the sofa lover, blankets, throws and cushions in cashmere, wool or merino are available for every pocket and make an ideal cosy winter gift.

- A posh hand soap, like the selection from *Jo Malone* presented in the iconic cream and black packaging, is almost unbeatable.

SECRET SANTA AND STOCKINGS

Don't panic about Secret Santa or filling a stocking. Both are easy to solve with a bit of left-field thinking.

- ❄ If the budget is small on this then how about a scratch card, *Lush* bath bomb or packet of garden seeds.

- ❄ As a big fan of battery-operated fairy lights, I think they make a great Secret Santa present, as does a disco light bulb that can transform any room into an instant dance floor.

- ❄ An *Opinel* pocket knife is perfect for the adventurer, as well as a thermos flask and head torch.

- ❄ Go wintry with a bobble hat or put extra love in and make a Christmas cake (like my one on page 36).

- ❄ I always love to give a novelty present like a crazy pair of slippers, but then balance it out with a book like *A Christmas Carol* by Charles Dickens.

- ❄ People of every age love a *LEGO* kit to build, or a new board game to play over Christmas.

- ❄ *Dobble* card game has lots of different themes, as does our old family favourite, *Monopoly*.

- ❄ And how about a pair of roller blades or a skateboard poking out of the top of a stocking?!

BEAUTY, BATH AND BODY

Beauty is one of my favourite subjects so I have come up with my top recommendations for the girls (and boys) in your lives.

- ❄ *Clinique's Sonic Brush* to cleanse the face is a godsend and one of my crucial bits of kit.

- ❄ I use *Origins Ginger Souffle* throughout the winter and swear by *Charlotte Tilbury's Magic Cream* – I like to buy both as gifts because I know they work for me.

- ❄ We all have trouble sleeping sometimes, so a pillow spray is a thoughtful choice.

- ❄ Beards are big (my dad's literally is) so a grooming kit including a comb and beautifully smelling moisturising oil is a good choice.

- ❄ A seriously good hairdryer sounds dull but can be a game changer.

- ❄ I can't not give my Christmas cosmetics collection a mention as I use it and give it as presents every year, with my Shimmer Body Cream being a big hit.

- ❄ If you are looking for something little, then a lip balm, tangle-teaser hairbrush, bath set or oil (*Aromatherapy Associates* are heaven) is the cutest little treat.

Dog Biscuits

Makes about 60, depending on your cutter size
Prep time: 20 minutes
Cooking time: 30 minutes

2 reduced-salt beef stock cubes
340g wholewheat flour, plus extra for dusting
80g skimmed dried milk powder
1 large egg, beaten
125ml vegetable oil

You will need a bone-shaped cookie cutter.

As I was testing recipes for this book I knew I couldn't leave my baby Martha Moo out. I love doing special things for her and I know she appreciates a gift, too. These make the cutest present for any canine friends you want to spoil.

Preheat the oven to 150°C/300°F/gas mark 2. Line 2 or 3 baking trays with baking parchment.

Put the beef stock cubes in a heatproof jug or bowl and add 150ml boiling water. Stir until the stock cubes have dissolved and allow to cool.

Combine the flour, milk powder, egg and oil in a bowl, then pour in the cooled beef stock. Mix to form a rough dough.

Dust the work surface with flour. Knead the dough on the work surface for 1–2 minutes until it comes together to form a smooth dough, then dust the surface again and roll it out to a thickness of about 1cm. Cut out about 60 biscuits with the cookie cutter, re-rolling the dough as necessary and arranging them on the lined baking trays as you go.

Bake the dog biscuits in the oven for 30 minutes. Remove from the oven and allow to cool before giving them to your favourite pooch. Keep them in the fridge in an airtight container for up to 2 weeks.

Florentines

Makes 24
Prep time: 20 minutes
Cooking time: 20 minutes

50g unsalted butter
20g plain flour
150g caster sugar
130ml double cream
50g whole almonds (skin
   on), roughly chopped
150g flaked almonds
100g chopped candied peel
50g glacé cherries, chopped
300g dark chocolate (70%
   cocoa solids), broken
   into chunks

I always love a recipe that can be flexible depending on the situation, and these Florentines are a good example. Make them as after-dinner petits fours, a teatime treat or bag them up, wrap with a bow and give as a sweet gift. I would be very happy to receive these.

Preheat the oven to 180°C/350°F/gas mark 4. Line a large baking sheet with baking parchment.

Put the butter, flour and sugar in a small saucepan and heat gently over a low heat until the butter has melted and combined with the flour. Slowly pour in the cream, stirring all the time, then add the chopped and flaked almonds, candied peel and chopped cherries. Stir well to combine, remove from the heat and leave the mixture to rest for a few minutes.

Scoop teaspoonfuls of the mixture onto the lined baking sheet, spacing them about 3cm apart so that they don't stick together while baking. To give them proper space, you may have to bake the Florentines in several batches (you should have enough mixture for 24 Florentines in total).

Flatten each one slightly and pop into the oven to bake for 10–14 minutes, or until they are flat and golden brown. Remove from the oven and leave them to set and harden on the baking sheet for 2–3 minutes, then transfer them to a wire rack to cool completely.

Melt the dark chocolate in a heatproof bowl set over a pan of simmering water, making sure that the bottom of the bowl doesn't touch the water, stirring occasionally until smooth. Flip the cooled Florentines upside down on the wire rack, and spoon over the melted chocolate to coat the back of each biscuit. Just before the chocolate hardens, use a fork to make wavy lines in each, then leave them to cool and set. They will keep in a cool place for up to a week so it is best to make them just before you want to give them as gifts.

Red Onion Chutney

Makes about 750g (enough
to fill 3 x 250g jars)
Prep time: 20 minutes
Cooking time: 1 hour
15 minutes

75ml olive oil
1.5kg red onions, peeled
and finely sliced
150g demerara sugar
50g soft light brown sugar
50g sweet chilli sauce
200ml cider vinegar
50ml balsamic vinegar
1 tsp salt
½ tsp black pepper

This is a savoury marmalade to accompany your Baked Camembert (pages 44–5), ham (page 244) or give as a handmade gift to a dear friend. Store it in jars and it will last throughout the season. Make some pretty labels (maybe like the ones on page 96) so it looks good on your table or on someone else's.

Heat the oil in a heavy-based saucepan over a medium heat. Add the sliced onions, stir a few times to coat them in the oil, then cover with a lid, turn down the heat to low, and leave for about 30 minutes, stirring occasionally. You want the onions to soften and begin to colour.

Add both the sugars and the sweet chilli sauce, turn up the heat to medium, remove the lid and cook for a further 30 minutes, until most of the moisture has cooked away and the onions are a deep rich brown colour.

Take the pan off the heat, and allow to cool for a few minutes then add both the vinegars. Return to the heat for a further 10–15 minutes, until the mixture becomes very sticky and thick.

Remove from the heat, season with the salt and pepper, stir, then pour into sterilised jars (see equipment on page 158). Seal and store in a cool, dark place for up to 1 year. Once opened, keep in the fridge for up to 1 month.

DIY Photo Album

You will need:

photos
glue or photo corners
a pretty hardback book
pens to write your
    messages

_____

This is such a personal gift and works for family and friends alike. I have used a shop-bought photo album for around £10 so it is an affordable present. You can go to town on the decoration, include little notes and drawings and stick in real photos.

❄ Decide which photos you are going to use on each page and stick them in using glue or photo corners.

❄ On the facing page, write a personal message, but make sure the pen has dried completely before you close the page!

DIY Orange and Ginger Body Scrub

Makes 1 x 500g jar

You will need:

pared zest of 1 orange
5cm piece of fresh ginger,
    peeled and thickly
    sliced
4 tbsp coconut oil
4 tbsp olive oil
10 drops of orange
    essential oil
150g raw cane sugar
130g coarse sea salt

This body scrub is such a great craft to give as a gift, or keep a big jar of it for yourself. I find it very therapeutic to make, and the combined orange and ginger scent instantly makes me feel festive. It's the perfect way to spoil dry, winter-battered skin.

Put the orange zest and ginger in a small saucepan with the coconut oil and olive oil. Warm gently over a low heat until the coconut oil melts, then warm through for 5 minutes. Swirl the pan occasionally. Do not let it boil. Remove from the heat and strain through a small sieve into a heatproof jug. Let the mixture drain for at least 15 minutes. Leave to cool to room temperature, then stir in the essential oil.

Mix together the sugar and salt in a bowl. Pour the infused oil mixture over the salt-sugar mixture and stir well.

Transfer to a clean jar, tie a festive ribbon around the neck of the jar and screw the lid on tightly. Use within 3 weeks.

Wrapping, Boxes and Bows

It is so exciting to be given a present wrapped in gorgeous paper, with a pretty wide ribbon tied in a big bow and a label peeking out with your name on it! I really appreciate a beautifully presented gift so I always want to do the same when I give mine – I think what is on the outside counts just as much as what is on the inside.

I like to get organised with wrapping papers, labels and decorations early in the month. I also get together scissors, ribbons, *Sellotape*, glue, gold pens and anything else I will need to hand so that I can set up a wrapping station in the kitchen or on the sitting room floor. It is nice to feel Christmassy, so pop *The Grinch* on while you work, or sing along to those festive hits and mull some wine to keep you going!

I get completely carried away with choosing a theme each year. Whether I go for metallic, patterned, simple or glittery, wrapping depends on my mood. Whatever I decide, I make sure I also have boxes and bags for certain presents, as well as tissue paper which is great for things without sharp edges. When it comes to stocking presents, we have a tradition in our family that we use big rolls of cheap and cheerful wrapping paper in bright colours, like kids' paper. There is no guilt when we rip through that on Christmas morning!

As a big fan of brown paper, I love wrapping that incorporates stencils of iconic Christmas images like snowmen, snowflakes and Christmas trees. In this chapter I show you how to create your very own version using brilliant stamps from *The English Stamp Company*. Stamp your labels to match and write on them with gold, silver or white pen for a chic, stylish finish.

Every present looks its best done up with a bow, whether it is with velvet, tartan or satin ribbon. Or string in brown or red and white stripe. As well as looking gorgeous it's good to have something to tie the label to, and you can use it to tuck in an extra treat or decoration. Maybe a sprig of winter foliage against the brown paper parcel, a candy cane tucked behind red ribbon against a wrapping covered in jolly Santas, or tie a cute Christmas decoration to it as an added gift.

Like much of my advice in this book, try not to leave the wrapping to the last minute. It is a bit of a family tradition in my house but I tend to wrap a couple of weeks before the day, particularly as I see friends throughout the month so need to give some presents early. It is also a good way to know if you have forgotten anyone, and that is not a panic I want on Christmas Eve!

DIY Wrapping Paper and Labels

You will need:

Christmas stamps
    (you could match
    the wrapping paper
    to your cards!)
rolls of brown paper
ink pads in different
    colours
brown gift labels
ribbons or string

Part of the joy I have in finding the right gift for someone is in the wrapping of it. The thought counts in the way you present it, not just in the gift itself, so I want it to look as beautiful and unique as possible. This is also a great craft to do on a night in with friends or when you are watching a film, and is often cheaper than shop-bought wrapping. If you suddenly run out of this you can just make some more!

❄ Take the stamp of your choice and press it into the ink pad, making sure it is evenly coloured with ink. It's a good idea to test the stamp out on some scrap paper so you get used to using it.

❄ Now for the fun bit! Unroll your brown paper to its full extent on a flat surface like a table or floor. Secure at both ends with a book or something to weight it down so it doesn't try to roll back up again.

❄ Stamp across the paper in whatever way you think looks pretty. If you want to do straight lines, then it's a good idea to draw very faint pencil marks across the paper so you keep everything evenly spaced. Leave the paper to dry and don't be tempted to roll it back up too soon as it will smudge if the ink is still wet. When it's properly dry you can rub out any pencil lines very gently.

❄ Lay out all your brown gift labels and use the same stamp you used for the paper, to make them match!

CHAPTER FOUR
Let's Party

Let's Party

I love a party. Whether I go as a guest or organise my own, my Christmas isn't complete without one. Jim and I always throw a big party the weekend before Christmas. It's the loveliest way to get all our family, friends and work gang together to celebrate the season which we all get excited about and look forward to every year!

In this chapter I take you through every aspect of organising a party, from creating a festive atmosphere through to the morning after the night before. I get so excited about the canapés and cocktails, putting together Christmassy and party hit playlists, tweaking my decorations and upping the fairy light and candle quota. The recipes I have included here are my absolute classic party pleasers which I serve every year without fail. Be prepared to be amazed by my Crostini 3 Ways (pages 112–114)!

I have also shared my definitive party outfits with you, as well as hair and makeup tutorials, to give a bit of help and inspiration. Getting ready to party is one of the highlights of the evening, especially if you are in front of the mirror with friends. I have a few of my closest friends arrive early and we all get ready together in my bedroom before I need to be at the door greeting guests. It's always a bit mad, but so fun with a bottle of fizz on the go, helping to curl each other's hair and about ten outfit changes each. The girls often end up wearing something from my wardrobe.

So, make sure you have factored in a bit of pampering in your schedule and be ready to greet your guests, looking as fabulous as they do.

Above all else, remember to enjoy the evening. As the host, you need to keep some sort of responsibility for the night, but this is about having a brilliant time too, so a bit of fun delegation always works. And as a guest it is good to offer a helping hand, top up drinks, hand around some sausage rolls and introduce yourself to people you haven't met before.

At my parties I always get a bit emotional when I look around and see everyone mingling – my mum speaking to one of my work team, friends fussing over my dog Martha and Jim checking everyone has a drink. It is the one time of year where all the different areas of my life come together and a moment for me to feel super thankful for everything I have. So don't be afraid, let's plan a party!

Perfect Party Planning

I don't think it is any secret that I am quite an organised person. So when it comes to planning a party I do start thinking about it way in advance. December is also the busiest month of the year so it's good to let your guests know as early as you can. In the past I have sent a 'save the date' email out three months before and then an official invitation nearer the time.

I pick a date for the week before Christmas when everyone is beginning to wind down from work and can see the holiday ahead. I like to choose a Friday night as it's a great way to end the week and kick-start the weekend, and friends can head straight over after work. I take the day off to get all the prep done, with help from Jim and any passing friends I can rope in.

Once you have set the date and designed invitations (making sure you include all the crucial information such as day, time, address, dress code and way to RSVP), draw up a guest list. Think about how much space you have and an idea of budget. I tend to invite around 50 people, which works for the sort of party I enjoy having. Not everyone will be able to make it (even with early 'save the date' prompts) but there are always additional people who join in. As a host, I know how important it is to let someone know if you can make their party so as a guest I always try to RSVP on time.

Your budget for the event is key so don't get carried away and book entertainment, plan to cover the garden with fake snow or set up a Santa's Grotto! As fantastic as this sounds, what everyone really wants is a fun night with their friends. Your cash should be spent on ingredients for delicious nibbles, drinks and a bit of sparkle to set the scene. Don't be afraid to ask guests to bring a bottle. Or wear a Christmas jumper. One year, my dad arrived with the best beard baubles I have ever seen – he looked fantastic. My friend Joe also always makes an effort and had turned up in a crazy flashing jumper!

I make a big party list of things to do and try to get as much done ahead of time as I can. The house has already been decorated but I may pick up some extra candles, hand soap for the loo, paper napkins and glittery table confetti.

Check you have enough glasses, or even better, hire them from your local supermarket or off licence. Plan what drinks you are going to serve and check you have enough space to chill bottles. Put your menu plan together and order anything that you think you won't be able to get hold of easily on the day. Make sure you have enough big plates and boards to serve the food on and some festive-themed paper plates for everyone to save on washing up.

Okay. I think you are just about ready to throw a party…

Eat, Drink and Be Merry

The day of the party has arrived! I always wake up with such a feeling of excitement, similar to Christmas morning. I know I have a long day of prepping and cooking ahead but I love every single second of it. The day goes very quickly, so keep an eye on your timings and try not to get too distracted.

As organised as I am, I do like to do a party food shop on the day. I know this sounds quite stressful but it is one of the fun parts of the build-up for me and I often come back with treats I hadn't thought of. Like one year, my friend Kate came shopping too and we got waylaid in the supermarket by a panettone tasting. We came home with the most delicious cake that got shared later at the party.

After a big food shop I come straight home, grab my apron, put the kettle on and get cooking. There are so many favourite recipes I wanted to include in this chapter but I have settled on those that I can't be without or that remind me of great party times. I love to cook throughout the afternoon and pop batches of Parmesan Stars (page 108), Sausage Rolls (page 110) and Mince Pies (page 158) in the oven. Jim borrows my apron and gets stuck in too, and I involve any friends or family who arrive early. It all adds to the party atmosphere and it is so fun to have them helping, even if they don't really know what they are doing. Like one year, my manager and good friend Georgia was helping me by brushing egg onto the top of mince pies to get them oven ready. She had never done it before so that year we had a batch of mince pies with a frittata topping!

Whatever you do, don't run out of time to get ready. How you look for your guests and yourself can just as easily set the tone of the evening as the music can. If you look like you are ready to party, everyone else is instantly in the mood. If you greet them at the door looking harassed, hair untouched, no makeup and in tracksuit bottoms, it gives the wrong message! Actually, getting ready feels like the start of the party for me if I have a glass of prosecco and a friend or two with me. Sitting on the floor, doing our makeup together, discussing the night ahead and trying on clothes is the best beginning to a party.

Leave yourself enough time to lay out the food and decorate the table. There won't be much space for a table centrepiece but always try to squeeze on some candles, confetti and a small bunch of white flowers. As well as the homemade treats like my deliciously topped Crostini (page 112), trio of Dips (pages 115–6) and I am most proud of my Ultimate Cheeseboard (page 120). It is always the showstopper at every party, covered with loads of different cheeses, pears, crackers and pickles – we cannot have a party without it! My friends Vanessa, Kieran, Maddie and George refuse to leave it all evening.

We also cannot have a party without a few celebratory cocktails. Or even an entire cocktail bar which we have had for the last couple of Christmas events. The barman loves coming to the parties and invents the most delicious cocktails with suitably festive names. You don't need to go the whole hog and get someone in. We often set up our own bar in the corner of the kitchen, fill the sink with ice, make the first round and then everyone takes it in turns to make more. As a guest I love stepping in for a round of cocktail making and like to come up with a twist on a classic. The drinks recipes I have included in this chapter (pages 122–5) are inspired by that.

Music is, of course, key to the atmosphere and how the party starts and continues. I greet everyone with some classic schmaltzy Christmas hits for the first hour or so. Once everyone is there and the noise levels and laughter rise, I swap playlists and put on chart music to dance to.

By the end of the evening I don't want it to end! The only way to solve this is to arrange a massive sleepover at your house like I did last year. Lots of my friends stayed over after the party and my parents popped around the corner to a lovely B&B. It makes me so happy when we all wake up together, girls still wearing their makeup from the night before, taking it slowly, after big mugs of tea, cuddling Martha and catching up on all the party gossip. My parents come back round to join us and we all cook a massive fry up with bacon, eggs, baked beans and mushrooms and stuff floury buns with whatever combination we fancy. There are always friends popping back the next day to collect random things they have left (one year Georgia went home without her handbag). My friends Emma and Hamish don't move from my sofa and I have to clear up around them before I join them and collapse in front of the TV for the rest of the day!

My Top Ten
Christmas Songs

'Last Christmas' - Wham

'All I Want For Christmas Is You' - Mariah Carey

'Christmas (Baby Please Come Home)' - Michael Bublé

'White Christmas' - Otis Redding

'Merry Christmas Everybody' - Slade

'I Wish It Could Be Christmas Every Day' - Wizzard

'Christmas Wrapping' - The Waitresses

'Santa Claus Is Coming To Town' - Jackson 5

'Driving Home For Christmas' - Chris Rea

'Happy Xmas (War is Over)' - John Lennon

Parmesan Stars

Makes about 15, depending on the size of your cutter
Prep time: 10 minutes
Cooking time: 12 minutes

125g grated hard cheese (I use Parmesan, because I love the flavour, but you could use a mix of Cheddar and Parmesan, if you prefer)
100g plain flour, plus extra for dusting
2 tsp baking powder
1½ tsp sweet paprika
100g cold unsalted butter, cubed
2 egg yolks

You will need a star-shaped cookie cutter.

These are cheese biscuit heaven. They always remind me of my friend Kate, as we visit her family every Christmas. Her mum serves a pile of these with prosecco and ginger liqueur cocktails and we exchange gifts. Heaven!

Preheat the oven to 220°C/425°F/gas mark 7. Line a baking sheet with baking parchment.

Put the grated cheese in a bowl. Sift over the flour, baking powder and paprika. Rub the butter into the flour and cheese with your fingertips until the mixture has a crumbly texture. You could also do this in a food processor: tip the grated cheese, dry ingredients and cubed butter into the bowl of the processor and pulse a few times until crumbly, then transfer the mixture to a bowl.

Add the egg yolks and mix with a spoon to combine and form a firm dough, then shape the dough into a ball. Dust the work surface with flour and roll out the dough to a thickness of 1cm. Cut out star shapes with the cookie cutter and arrange them on the lined baking sheet.

Bake the cheese stars at the top of the oven for 8–12 minutes until light golden brown, then remove from the oven and leave to cool on the sheet.

Sausage Rolls

Makes 20 mini rolls
Prep time: 45 minutes
Cooking time: 25 minutes

450g self-raising flour, plus
    extra for dusting
1 tsp salt
75g cold unsalted butter
    or margarine, cubed
150g cold vegetable fat,
    suitable for baking,
    cubed
6 sausages
milk, for brushing

It wouldn't be Christmas Eve without a batch of these baking in the oven. We make them every year and I use my nanny's recipe with self-raising flour rather than plain, as our family prefers a softer pastry. I don't add anything fancy, but if I am making them for a big party, I sometimes use ready-made pastry to save time.

Put the flour and salt in a large bowl and add the butter and vegetable fat. Use your fingertips to work the fats into the flour until it is crumbly. Drizzle in about 7 tablespoons of cold water and, with your hands, bring the mixture together to form a soft dough. Tip the dough out onto a work surface dusted with flour and press it into a disc. Wrap in clingfilm and chill in the fridge for 30 minutes.

While the dough is chilling, slip the sausagemeat out of its casings and put the meat in a bowl. Separate it into 2 mounds. Preheat the oven to 200°C/400°F/gas mark 6. Line a baking tray with baking parchment.

Once the dough has chilled, unwrap it and roll it out on the floured work surface to a rectangle roughly 30 x 20cm and about 5mm thick, with the long edge facing you.

Take half the sausagemeat and lay it in one long log along the long side of the pastry facing you, about 2.5cm from the edge. Roll the sausagemeat up in the pastry, and when the pastry has made its way around the whole log (using half the width of the rectangle), trim the pastry along the length of the log. Repeat with the other half of the meat and pastry. Cut into 4–5cm-thick slices and place on the lined baking tray. Using a pastry brush, brush the tops with milk and pop into the oven to bake for 25 minutes, or until golden brown. Remove from the oven and cool a little on a wire rack before eating, but they're best eaten warm.

Crostini 3 Ways

Each variation makes
   about 20
Prep time for each:
   10 minutes
Cooking time for each:
   15 minutes (plus extra
   roasting and resting time
   for the beef)

1 baguette
extra-virgin olive oil, for
   drizzling or brushing
1 garlic clove

6–8 fresh ripe figs
2 logs of soft goats' cheese
runny honey

290g jar of black pitted
   Kalamata olives, drained
   (160g drained weight)
100g sun-dried tomatoes in
   olive oil
100g cherry tomatoes
½ small bunch of fresh basil
salt and pepper

There is something for everyone in these three versions of my crostini, a sure-fire canapé hit at a party. You make the same toasted garlic-smeared bread base for each, then all you have to do is pile on different toppings.

Preheat the oven to 200ºC/400ºF/gas mark 6.

Cut the baguette into 5mm-thick diagonal slices (you should get about 20 slices) and lay the slices on a baking tray. Drizzle or brush them with olive oil and pop in the oven for 10–15 minutes, or until they're toasty and golden, turning them once halfway through.

As soon as they're out of the oven, cut the garlic clove in half and rub the slices of baguette with the cut side of the clove to give them a slight garlicky flavour.

GOATS' CHEESE AND FIG

Cut the fresh figs in half from stem to base, then slice them into thin wedges.

Cut the logs of goats' cheese into 5mm-thick slices (about 10 slices per log). Top the warm crostini with a slice of goats' cheese and a wedge or two of fig. Arrange on a platter and drizzle lightly with honey.

CHOPPED TOMATO AND OLIVE

Roughly chop the olives on a board and tip them into a bowl. Do the same with the sun-dried tomatoes, tipping them into the bowl with the olives. Cut the cherry tomatoes into eighths and add them to the bowl, too. Pick off the larger leaves of basil and stack them on your board. Keep the pretty smaller leaves to one side for decoration. Slice the stack of leaves into thin ribbons and toss them into the bowl. Drizzle over about 1 tablespoon of oil from the sun-dried tomato jar, and stir the mixture to combine. Season with salt and pepper, top the warm crostini with the mixture and garnish with the small basil leaves.

recipe continued overleaf

750g–1kg boneless beef joint
(topside is best, but rump
would do the trick, too)
4–6 tbsp olive oil, plus
1 tsp for the beef
2 tbsp capers, drained
2 garlic cloves
4 anchovy fillets in oil
1 medium bunch of fresh
flat-leaf parsley (about
50g), leaves only
½ bunch of fresh basil, leaves
only (about 12g)
½ bunch of fresh mint, leaves
only (about 12g)
½ bunch of fresh dill
(about 12g)
1 tsp English mustard
1 tbsp red wine vinegar
salt and pepper

BEEF AND SALSA VERDE

This is almost certainly more beef that you'll need for 1 baguette's worth of crostini canapés, but it doesn't make sense to cook a joint of beef any smaller than this. Plus, cold beef is never a bad thing to have in the fridge…

Take the beef out of the fridge at least 1 hour before you want to cook it. Preheat the oven to 190°C/375°F/gas mark 5.

Pat the beef dry with kitchen paper, and place it in a small roasting tin. Pour about a teaspoon of olive oil into the palm of your hand and rub it all over the joint. Season the meat with plenty of pepper and a little salt.

Pop the beef in the oven and roast it for 13 minutes per 450g for medium rare – so you need to give a 1kg joint about 28 minutes. If you prefer it cooked well done, allow 16 minutes per 450g.

Once the time is up, take it out of the oven, transfer it to a board or plate, and cover it with foil to rest for 30 minutes. You can serve the beef warm or cold, so after the 30 minutes of resting, you could pop it in the fridge to slice and serve later on.

To make the salsa verde, put the capers, garlic and anchovies in a food processor or blender and blitz a few times then add all the herbs, mustard and red wine vinegar. Whizz everything together, and while the motor is running, slowly pour in the olive oil. Stop to scrape down the sides, add a crack of black pepper and whizz one final time. It should be the consistency of pesto. If you don't have a food processor, simply chop the ingredients finely by hand and combine them in a bowl.

Once the beef has rested, slice it as thinly as possible. Top each crostini with half a slice of beef and about a teaspoon of salsa verde.

Tip: If you have any left over, salsa verde is a very versatile sauce – it's delicious with roasted or poached fish and is a fancy alternative to mint sauce with lamb.

Dips with Crudités

These are satisfying to make and so much tastier than bought dips. I would encourage you to make all three (especially the beetroot hummus, for its gorgeous festive colour). Put them out on the table with bowls of raw veg (cut into sticks or left whole), tortilla chips, crisps and bread sticks to scoop them up. They make a great party-table dish, too.

Prep time: 10 minutes
Cooking time: 40 minutes

4 white onions
2 tbsp olive oil
1 tbsp balsamic vinegar
1 x 400g tin cannellini
    beans, drained and
    rinsed
juice of 2 lemons
2 garlic cloves, roughly
    chopped
3 tbsp plain natural yoghurt
small bunch of fresh
    flat-leaf parsley, leaves
    only
salt and pepper

WHITE BEAN AND ROASTED ONION DIP

Preheat the oven to 180°C/350°F/gas mark 4.

Peel the onions, cut them into wedges and chuck them into a bowl. Drizzle with the olive oil and balsamic vinegar and season generously with salt and pepper. Tip the onions into a roasting tin and pop into the oven for 25 minutes to roast.

After the onions have been roasting for 25 minutes, add the drained and rinsed beans to the roasting tin with the onions, and give everything a shake. Roast for a further 10–15 minutes, until the onions are nice and soft and the juices have caramelised.

Take the tin out of the oven and allow the beans and onions to cool slightly, then tip the whole lot into the bowl of your food processor or blender. Add the lemon juice, garlic, yoghurt and parsley leaves. Blitz to a coarse paste and taste for seasoning. Spoon into a bowl or container and chill, bringing it out to come to room temperature before serving.

recipes continued overleaf

Prep time: 15 minutes
Cooking time: 60 minutes

500g beetroot (roughly
    5 medium beetroot), peeled
    and cut into rough cubes
1 tbsp olive oil
1 tbsp tahini
200g tinned chickpeas
    (half a 400g tin),
    drained and rinsed
    (keep some of the
    liquid from the tin)
juice of ½ lemon
2 garlic cloves
½ tsp ground cumin
salt and pepper

Prep time: 5 minutes

small bunch of fresh flat-leaf
    parsley (leaves and stems)
small bunch of fresh chives
small bunch fresh basil
    (leaves only)
small bunch of fresh tarragon
1 small garlic clove (optional)
3 tbsp sour cream
300g mayonnaise
pinch of cayenne pepper
salt and pepper

BEETROOT HUMMUS

Preheat the oven to 180°C/350°F/gas mark 4.

Put the cubed beetroot in a small roasting tin with the olive oil, a sprinkling of salt and pepper and a splash of water.

Roast into the oven for 45 minutes–1 hour, giving them a little toss halfway through, until the beetroot is soft. Remove from the oven and allow to cool slightly.

Tip the roasted beetroot and all the remaining ingredients into the bowl of your food processor or blender and blitz to a fine paste. If it's too thick, add a little of the reserved chickpea tin water to loosen. Taste and adjust the seasoning and/or add more lemon, if you like.

Spoon into a bowl or container and chill, bringing it out to come to room temperature before serving.

HERBY DIP

Put the herbs in the bowl of your food processor or blender with the garlic (if using) and pulse a few times then add the sour cream and mayonnaise. Blitz to combine, then add a pinch of salt, a few grinds of black pepper and the cayenne pepper. Spoon into a bowl or container and chill in the fridge until ready to serve.

Smoked Salmon
AND CREAM CHEESE BLINIS

Serves 8 (2 canapés each)
Prep time: 10 minutes

1 packet of shop-bought
    blinis (packet of 16)
50g cream cheese
200g smoked salmon slices,
    torn or cut in half
freshly ground black pepper
½ lemon

These are one of the simplest but most effective canapés as they are luxurious but so quick to prepare. I make sure I have the ingredients to hand so I can throw them together at the last minute. They also make a delicious Christmas Eve starter.

Reheat the blinis according to the instructions on the packet.

Once the blinis are warm, spread about a teaspoon of cream cheese on each one, and top with half a slice of smoked salmon. Arrange on a serving platter then sprinkle with pepper and squeeze the lemon over the lot.

Ultimate Cheeseboard

Serves 10–12
Prep time: 10 minutes

1 quarter wheel of brie or
   1 whole camembert
200g mature Cheddar
   cheese, preferably
   in wax
200g milder Cheddar
300g Stilton (or blue cheese
   of your choice)
1 whole Époisses or other
   very soft, washed rind
   cheese
200g gruyère or other
   mature hard cheese
200g hard or soft goats' or
   sheep cheese
150g Red Leicester
200g cranberry-studded
   Wensleydale
Lots of vegetables, fruit,
   bread and biscuits to go
   alongside, including:
   grapes
   small carrots
   pears
   apples
   figs
   Medjool dates
   crackers
   bread
   oatcakes
   chutneys
   honey

This makes the most amazing centrepiece on a Christmas party table. I have an enormous wooden board and, as well as including my favourite selection of cheeses, I pile on raw vegetables, fruit, crackers and jars of chutney or my Red Onion Chutney (page 88). I know this is an assembly rather than a recipe, but it is an integral part of our festivities so I had to include it.

Arrange the ingredients on a large board or platter.

Cocktails & Mocktails

GINGERBREAD ESPRESSO MARTINI

These go down so well at a party and combine all the deliciousness of Christmas in a glass.

Put all the ingredients for the gingerbread syrup in a small saucepan with 120ml water. Place over a medium-high heat and bring to the boil, stirring until the sugar has dissolved. Turn down the heat and simmer for 5 minutes. Remove from the heat and leave to cool completely before using. Strain and store in a sealed jar in the fridge for up to a month.

Combine the ingredients for the spiced sugar, then coat the rim of a martini glass (chill it first if you like) with the mixture.

In a cocktail shaker, shake the vodka, espresso and syrup together with a handful of ice cubes. Strain into the glass and garnish with the coffee beans.

Makes 1
50ml vodka
30ml chilled espresso coffee
30ml gingerbread syrup
    (see below)
ice cubes
3 coffee beans, to garnish

**For the gingerbread syrup
(makes about 150ml):**
100g caster sugar
3 cloves
1 cinnamon stick
thumb-sized piece of fresh
    ginger, peeled and sliced

For the spiced sugar:
2 tbsp golden caster sugar
½ tsp ground cinnamon
½ tsp freshly grated nutmeg

NEGRONI

I dedicate this to Jim as it is his ultimate cocktail. Serve in a short glass and enjoy.

Makes 1
25ml Campari
25ml vermouth rosso
25ml gin
ice cubes
strips of orange zest, to garnish

Pour the Campari, vermouth and gin into an Old Fashioned glass, add some ice cubes and stir gently to combine. Garnish with the strips of orange peel.

MOSCOW MULE

I was so impressed with the Soho House version of this which is served in copper mugs that I bought similar mugs for my own mules. This is one of my favourite cocktails.

Makes 1
75ml vodka
juice of 1 lime
175ml ginger beer
ice cubes
wedge of lime and a sprig
  of mint, to garnish

Pour the vodka, lime juice and ginger beer into a chilled mug (a copper one if you happen to have it) and stir. Add lots of ice cubes and garnish with the wedge of lime and sprig of mint.

LIMONCELLO SHOT

These create an instant party atmosphere and are a lovely winter take on a tequila slammer.

Makes 1
spiced sugar (see opposite),
  to coat the rim of the glass
35ml cold limoncello
orange wedge, to chase

Coat the rim of a chilled shot glass with spiced sugar and pour in the limoncello. Like doing a tequila shot, lick the rim of the glass before drinking the limoncello, then bite into the orange wedge to finish.

CLEMENTINE CRANBERRY BELLINI

This is my Christmas Day version of Buck's Fizz. They are so successful that there is always someone making the next one before you've finished the first.

Makes 1
25ml cranberry juice
25ml clementine juice
cold prosecco, Champagne, cava or sparkling
    wine, to serve

Pour the two juices into the bottom of a champagne flute or coupe and top with bubbly of your choice.

FESTIVE PINK GIN

Gin is a crowd pleaser, and there are so many to choose from. I like to go a bit Old School here and include a generous dash of angostura bitters which gives this the most beautiful subtle pinkish hue.

Makes 1
50ml gin
dash of angostura bitters
ice cubes
cold tonic water
sprig of rosemary, to garnish

Pour the gin into a tall glass, add the angostura bitters and some ice cubes and top up with tonic water. Stir gently to combine and garnish with the rosemary for a herby finish.

ELDERFLOWER FIZZ

This is such a refreshing non-alcoholic long drink. It looks just like a gin cocktail and is a welcome reminder of summer.

Makes 1
25ml elderflower cordial
juice of 1 lime
ice cubes
cold sparkling water
pared strips of lime and lemon zest, to garnish

Pour the elderflower cordial into a chilled tall glass, add the lime juice and some ice cubes, and top up with sparkling water. Stir gently and garnish with the strips of lime and lemon zest.

POMEGRANATE FIZZ

I adore the ruby jewel colour of this mocktail, and love using pomegranates, which are so popular at Christmas. Pomegranate juice is easy to source in the supermarket but it is great to get a fresh fruit so you can add the seeds for decoration. Apparently, the seeds represent coins and predict wealth for the year ahead!

Makes 1
50ml pomegranate juice
1 tbsp pomegranate seeds
ice cubes
lemonade
wedge of lime, to garnish

Pour the pomegranate juice into a chilled tall glass and add the pomegranate seeds. Add some ice cubes and top up with lemonade. Garnish with the lime wedge and watch the seeds dance in the bubbles of the lemonade.

Christmas Wardrobe

I like to get my Christmas outfits organised in advance and am always inspired by tweaks on the classics, using sumptuous winter fabrics like velvet, a bit of sparkle and a novelty Christmas jumper! Here I have put together four outfits for you guys that should get you through most festive occasions. I think anyone could pick from them and I've even tested them out on my friends – they all picked different ones so it's good to know there is something for everyone here. I personally love all four and would mix and match them depending on the party.

I love a short black dress with long sheer sleeves as it feels chic, and the velvet, heeled sandals with a simple toe and ankle strap are very elegant and luxurious.

Pairing a fun Christmas jumper with leather leggings and heels is the perfect way to give this outfit a fashionable edge and transform it into an evening look.

This is a strong, confident look which makes you instantly party ready, and the patent leather skirt is a wardrobe staple throughout the season.

A velvet jumpsuit is my idea of heaven! This outfit is a must throughout the season – it works for every occasion and is so comfortable it's like wearing pyjamas.

Christmas Looks

I have chosen two makeup and two hair tutorials that are fairly simple. I wanted to include them here as much for inspiration as for detailed explanation. It is really useful to have a couple of looks up your sleeve for a big night out and it ultimately saves time when you are getting ready.

My biggest piece of advice to you is that prep is key – give yourself a good old pamper before a party. In the winter, skin can easily end up looking tired, chalky pale and dry, so don't cut corners on your skincare routine. I indulge in everything from a relaxing face mask to massaging in a luxurious moisturiser to encourage my skin to look healthy. My current fave is *Charlotte Tilbury's Magic Cream* but there are lots of great products on the market and they don't need to be expensive. I think it is so much lovelier to have a skin radiating with creams and bronzer than with fake tan. Choose one of the following makeup looks and you will feel and look incredible.

SKIN

※ Use your foundation or tinted moisturiser and add in a blob of face illuminator (check it is photo friendly first and doesn't reflect camera flash), then mix them together on the back of your hand using a foundation brush. Apply to the skin starting at the centre and working your way out. You can even use your fingers for a more natural look.

※ Use a yellow toned concealer for any red spots or blemishes on your skin that still show through after using foundation/tinted moisturiser. Remember, you want your skin to look as natural as possible, and using a foundation that covers everything will be too heavy.

※ Use an under-eye concealer to get rid of any dark circles.

※ I tend to just powder the centre of my face with a translucent pressed powder (I prefer pressed as I can just throw it in my handbag to touch up throughout the night). If your skin is oilier you may wish to powder all over.

※ To add definition to your face, take a contour powder or contour cream stick and brush in the hollows of your cheekbones (suck in your cheeks to find them if they are not obvious – I have to do this!) and just under your chin and along your jawline.

※ For healthy-looking skin, use a large fluffy brush to add bronzer to all the high points of your face.

※ Finally, highlight by using either a powder or cream highlighter and just blend this onto the tops of your cheekbones. Now your skin will be looking completely gorgeous and glowing.

BROWS

Fill in your brows using either a powder or pencil. Brow shape is such a personal thing, but I love a fairly strong brow with quite straight lines. By this I mean I am not a fan of a rounded arch, so when filling in between points 1, 2 and 3 (see right), make the line from 1 to 2 straight and 2 to 3 straight (obviously within reason, not in an unnatural way!).

✻ Mark the three points using an eyebrow pencil. If you were to draw an imaginary line (or use a the handle of a brush as a guide) from the edge of your nose up through the inner corner of your eye, this is where the inner edge of your eyebrow (1) should roughly start.

✻ Now imagine a line that goes from the corner of your nose, through the middle of your eye: that's where the top of your arch should be (2) – but follow the natural shape of your brow so it suits your face! You want it to look real.

✻ The outer edge of your brow (3) should roughly be where an imaginary line would end if you were to draw one from the edge of your nose through the outer corner of your eye.

✻ My only tip with the actual filling-in part would be to use a light hand and try and be a little scruffy as you draw in the hairs; that way you'll end up with a more natural looking brow.

Makeup Look 1

THE FESTIVE GOLDEN SMOKY EYE

This look creates a gold and dark brown smoky eye with a nude lip and golden skin glow:

❄ Apply a peachy pink blush to the apples of your cheeks – you could use cream or powder, whichever you prefer! Then take your foundation brush and blend the blush at the edges so it looks seamless and not obvious.

❄ Use a gold-toned cream shadow base in order to get a real intensity with your eyeshadows. Blend this all over the lid and underneath your eyes.

❄ Use a gold metallic eyeshadow all over the lid and underneath on top of the cream shadow, and blend using a fluffy brush so you can't see exactly where the eyeshadow finishes and your eyelid without shadow on it begins. Don't blend over your entire lid or you'll just end up removing product; just blend the edges.

❄ Use a dark brown or black kohl eye pencil and pop this along your waterline and also scribble it into your top and bottom lash line. You'll need a more precise brush like a pencil brush to blend this at your lash line top and bottom.

❄ Give your lashes a good curl and add plenty of mascara top and bottom.

❄ Now just use a 'My Lips But Better'-style lipstick.

Makeup Look 2

THE CHRISTMAS RED LIP

This look combines a dramatic red lip with a nude eye and golden skin glow:

❄ Apply a bronzey-toned blush to the apples of your cheeks (I love a colour like this with a red lip: *MAC Warm Soul* would be perfect) and blend in the way I have explained in Look 1.

❄ Sweep a matte light brown shadow all over your lid and a medium brown shadow through your crease. Also sweep this one underneath your eyes. Keep it soft and blown out, blend it really well.

❄ Give your lashes a good curl and add plenty of mascara top and bottom.

❄ Line your lips using a liner that matches your red lipstick of choice. A good tip is to actually line your entire lips, not just the outside, because if you're drinking and eating at a party, it will last much longer and even if the lipstick wears off you'll still have the liner underneath! In this photo here I am using a red liquid lipstick and I actually line afterwards as I find it easier this way – but whatever works best for you!

❄ Now fill in your lips with a gorgeous red lipstick; the more matte in texture, the longer lasting it'll be.

Hair Look 1

THE PINNED-BACK LOOSE WAVES

Loose waves and taking back one or two pieces from the front:

❀ This style works with both freshly washed and second day hair. So, once your hair is dry (or it may already be dry if it's second day hair!) give it a good spritz with a heat protectant.

❀ Depending on the thickness of your hair, separate it into sections. I only have to do two sections as I don't have lots of hair!

❀ Now with each section, just take your time, taking 2.5cm sections at a time and wrapping them around your curling wand. Hold for about 10 seconds and release. Try to curl your hair in alternate directions for each section – this will achieve a more natural, casual wave.

❀ Once you've done this to all the sections of your hair, shake it out and give it a light spray of hairspray.

❀ Put one pump of nourishing hair oil into the palm of your hand and rub your hands together so the oil is evenly spread over your hands. Now just gently work it through the mid lengths and ends of your hair. This will ensure your hair looks healthy and glossy.

❀ Take a 5cm section from the top of your head at the parting and use a clip to hold it out of the way for the moment.

❀ Then, from the very front of your hairline take a 5cm section from one side.

❀ Starting at the parting, twist the section then lift it up towards the crown and pin in place.

❀ Finally, once you have secured the twist, let down the section from the top of your head to cover the grip as per the photo. Repeat on the other side if you would like it on both.

Hair Look 2

THE SLEEK LOW PONY TAIL

Slick low ponytail with deep side or centre parting for drama:

* Give your hair a spritz of serum to make it easy to achieve a slicked-back look.

* Choose your parting and use a comb to get it in a perfect line.

* Slick back your hair using a brush towards the nape of your neck (or just above) and secure with a hairband, leaving a 2.5cm section free.

* Wrap the loose part around the hairband and secure with a hair grip.

* Finish with a light squirt of hairspray to smooth any fly-away hairs.

CHAPTER FIVE

Christmas Baking

Christmas Baking

When I had the idea to write this book, the very first chapter I thought about with the most excitement was this one! Baking is a big part of my life and at Christmas it takes on a whole new meaning. I bake my way through December, making gifts and treats to share with my friends and give as presents. Putting a batch of my Iced, Spiced Scones (page 148) in the oven makes me feel instantly Christmassy.

I adore being in the kitchen, cooking and hanging out with friends. It's the perfect antidote to the more stressful side of the festive season. I often bake by myself when I am in need of a little therapeutic me-time. I stick on some relaxing Christmas music and make something quite tricky so that I can focus and zone out from the world around me. Baking can also be a fun group activity, too. I love blasting out 'Jingle Bell Rock' as my friends and I (covered in flour) re-enact the *Mean Girl*'s routine around the kitchen island.

The most difficult part of working on this section was choosing which recipes to include, as I started with way too many. It has really made me think about what types of food sum up Christmas for me and how crucial these dishes are to my yuletide happiness, like my nanny's Sausage Rolls (page 110), hot out of the oven on Christmas Eve, my sister Tash and I baking mince pies together, creatively decorating the annual chocolate Yule Log (page 166) or serving up a big spoonful of trifle (page 172). In my family, like so many

others, cooking and eating together is a big part of how we celebrate over Christmas. I wanted this book to convey exactly what we love to eat and why.

I am always tinkering with my recipes, taking old favourites and giving them a seasonal tweak. For the show-stopping White Chocolate Winter Wonderland Cake (page 164) I have used my definitive white chocolate sponge recipe from *Tanya Bakes* as a starting point and then taken it in a full-on festive direction! I really hope this chapter encourages you to try new things and gives you a bit of confidence that if I can do it, so can you. I had never made my own mincemeat before, and was not sure if it would work, but it couldn't have been easier!

As you know, I have a rather sweet tooth so, while there are lots of savoury recipes elsewhere in the book, I really wanted this part to focus on puddings, cakes, pies and bakes.

Some of these recipes have been inspired by an ingredient, flavour or person. Marshmallows that become a cute snowman face on top of a homemade biscuit (page 152) or the memory of a delicious brownie and salted caramel ice cream shared with good friends (page 178).

And the easiest part of writing this chapter… testing the recipes and eating the results!

Orange Chocolate Tear-and-share Cookie

Makes 3 big cookies
Prep time: 10 minutes
Cooking time: 16 minutes

200g unsalted butter, softened
300g caster sugar
1 large egg
320g self-raising flour
30g cocoa powder
a dash of milk (optional)
320g orange-flavoured chocolate, broken into roughly 2cm chunks

I love a big tear-and-share cookie and this one even looks like orange segments once it's cut! You don't have to use orange-flavoured chocolate though – you can use any chocolate you have in your Christmas cupboard. I'm looking forward to making these this Christmas with my friend Steffi, as we love making cookies together.

Preheat the oven to 200°C/400°F/gas mark 6. Line 2 baking trays with baking parchment.

Put the butter and sugar in a bowl and cream together until light and fluffy. Crack in the egg and incorporate it into the butter and sugar, then stir in the dry ingredients. Add a dash of milk if your mixture is looking dry.

Add the orange-flavoured chocolate chunks to the mixture, using your hands to incorporate them into the dough.

Roughly divide the dough into 3 and press a third of the dough into a disc about 1.5cm thick on one of the lined baking trays. Repeat with the remaining dough. If your trays are big enough, place 2 discs of dough on one tray, but be aware that the cookies will spread in the oven so don't place them close together. If your baking trays aren't quite big enough, bake the cookies in batches.

Pop the trays into the oven for 14 minutes, then take them out and, using a knife, score each cookie into 8 wedges before popping back in the oven for a further 2 minutes. Take them out and leave to cool on the trays for about 20 minutes before sharing. You could serve them warm, with a big scoop of ice cream on top and lots of spoons!

Isaac's Chocolate-dipped Shortbread

Makes about 18
Prep time: 15 minutes
Cooking time: 20 minutes

175g unsalted butter,
  softened
75g caster sugar
250g plain flour, plus extra
  for dusting
200g milk chocolate, broken
  into chunks

*You will need festive
cookie cutters.*

These are inspired by my nephew Isaac. One Christmas he offered me his own 'homemade' biscuits made from dipping shop-bought shortbread into melted chocolate. I have made this version just for him.

Line a baking tray (one that will fit in your fridge) with baking parchment.

Put the butter and sugar in a large bowl and beat with a wooden spoon until the mixture forms a pale paste. Add the flour and stir with the wooden spoon until you have a crumbly dough.

Dust the work surface with flour. Tip the mixture out onto the surface and, using your hands, bring the dough together into a disc about 1cm thick, pressing all the crumbly bits together.

Cut out 18 festive shapes, such as Christmas trees and snowmen, and carefully lay them on the lined baking tray. Transfer the tray of shapes to the fridge for 20 minutes to chill. Preheat the oven to 190°C/375°F/gas mark 5.

Pop the chilled tray of pastry shapes in the oven for 15–20 minutes, or until pale golden on top. Remove from the oven and leave them to firm up on the tray for a few minutes then transfer to a wire rack to cool completely.

Once the biscuits are cool, melt the chocolate in a heatproof bowl set over a pan of simmering water, making sure that the bottom of the bowl doesn't touch the water, stirring occasionally until smooth. Once the chocolate is melted and the biscuits are cool, dip them in the melted chocolate. Transfer them to a wire rack and leave them for 20 minutes to set (or pop them in the fridge to help the chocolate set faster).

Iced, Spiced Scones

Makes 8
Prep time: 10 minutes
Cooking time: 15 minutes

250g self-raising flour,
    plus extra for dusting
1 tsp baking powder
1 tsp ground cinnamon
¼ tsp freshly grated nutmeg
pinch of salt
40g unsalted butter,
    softened
30g golden caster sugar
1 large egg, lightly beaten
125ml milk, plus extra
    for brushing

For the glaze:
3–4 tbsp milk
150g icing sugar, sifted

*You will need a 5cm round
pastry cutter.*

This recipe is inspired by Gail's Bakery and the love I have for their scones. It doesn't need any butter or cream and jam accompaniment, just a big mug of tea in front of *Miracle on 34th Street*.

Preheat the oven to 200°C/400°F/gas mark 6. Line a baking tray with baking parchment.

Combine the flour, baking powder, spices and salt in a bowl, add the butter and, using your fingertips, work the butter into the flour until the mixture has a crumbly texture. Stir in the sugar.

Tip the lightly beaten egg into the flour mixture then add the milk, little by little, until you have a soft, sticky dough (you might not need all the milk).

Dust the work surface with flour, tip the dough out onto the surface and, using your hands, pat it into a flat disc. Roll it gently a few times to flatten it to a thickness of 2–3cm.

Using the 5cm cutter, cut out a circle and place it on the lined baking tray. Repeat, and when you need to bring your dough back together, knead it lightly, before patting into a disc to cut more circles (you should get a total of 8 circles).

Brush the tops with milk and pop in the oven for 10–12 minutes, or until the tops of the scones are golden.

While the scones bake, prepare the glaze by stirring the milk into the icing sugar a little at a time until you have a smooth, pourable mixture. Set aside.

Remove the scones from the oven and transfer to a wire rack to cool completely. Pour the glaze over the tops and allow to set, or devour whilst still runny.

Mini Crispy Christmas Puddings

Makes 24
Prep time: 10 minutes, plus
40 minutes setting time
Decorating time: 20 minutes

50g salted butter, plus extra
for greasing
300g mini marshmallows
150g puffed rice cereal
300g dark chocolate (70%
cocoa solids), broken
into chunks
icing sugar, for dusting
red, white and green
ready-rolled icing

You will need small holly-shaped cutters, or a small sharp knife.

Puffed rice cakes just got Christmassy. They are always popular with the children but adults can't resist them either. Take your time when you're decorating them, for a fabulous end result.

Line a baking tray or plate that will fit in your fridge with baking parchment. Melt the butter in a saucepan over a medium heat.

Tip in the marshmallows and stir constantly with a heatproof plastic or rubber spatula until the mixture is fully melted and smooth. Take off the heat and stir in the puffed rice. Mix with a spatula until well combined.

While the mixture is still warm, rub butter onto your clean hands and scoop out small balls. Roll them into spheres about the size of golf balls and place them on the lined baking tray or plate. Re-grease your hands with butter and continue with the rest of the mixture until you have 24 balls.

Pop the tray or plate in the fridge for 20 minutes, to allow the 'puddings' to firm up.

Meanwhile, melt the chocolate in a heatproof bowl set over a pan of simmering water, making sure that the bottom of the bowl doesn't touch the water, stirring occasionally until smooth. Remove from the heat.

Once the balls have firmed up, dip them one by one into the melted chocolate, turning them with two forks to coat them completely. Transfer them to a wire rack set over a baking tray to catch the drips. Once you've coated them all evenly, pop them back in the fridge (on the rack) to set.

While the balls are chilling, dust the work surface with icing sugar and roll out some white icing. Cut out 24 small rough circles, about 4cm in diameter, and set them to one side. Roll out some green icing and, using a shaped cutter or small knife, cut out 48–60 small holly shapes and set them to one side. Then pinch off small amounts of red icing and roll them in your hands to make 24 tiny 'holly berry' balls, about 5mm in diameter.

Remove the balls from the fridge and, wetting the backs of the white icing circles with a tiny bit of water to help them stick, top each ball with a white icing disc, then add 2 or 3 holly leaves and a berry.

Melting Snowman Cookies

Makes 20
Prep time: 10 minutes
Cooking time: 15 minutes
Decorating time: 20 minutes

For the biscuits:
110g caster sugar
225g unsalted butter,
    softened
275g plain flour, plus extra
    for dusting

For the icing:
200g icing sugar
3–4 tbsp milk

To decorate:
ready-made writing icing in
    tubes (a few different
    colours)
20 mini marshmallows
orange jelly slices, or other
    jellied orange sweet
mini chocolate chips or
    chocolate-coated puffed
    rice

*You will need a 7cm round
pastry cutter.*

Whatever your age, you will appreciate these cute cookies. The biscuits are easy to make and the fun is in the decorating. It's a brilliant edible crafts project for children to enjoy tackling, too. I am obsessed with marshmallows so these little faces make me very happy.

Preheat the oven to 180°C/350°F/gas mark 4. Line 2 baking sheets with baking parchment.

Put the sugar and butter in a bowl and cream together until thick and pale. Stir in the flour until everything is mixed together.

Dust the work surface with flour. Tip the mixture out onto the surface and work it into a disc with your hands, gathering in all the crumbly bits as you go and working them into a dough. Roll out the dough to a thickness of 5mm then cut out 20 circles with the 7cm cutter, re-rolling scraps of dough as necessary and arranging them on the lined baking sheets as you go.

Bake the cookies in the oven for 13–15 minutes, or until they are golden brown. Leave on the tray to firm up for a few minutes then transfer to a wire rack and leave to cool completely.

While waiting for the cookies to cool, decorate your snowmen's faces by using writing icing in tubes to draw eyes and a mouth on individual marshmallows. Use orange jelly slices cut into tiny wedges for a carrot nose. Allow the decorated faces to set.

Make the icing by sifting the icing sugar into a bowl and stirring in the milk little by little until you have a thick, smooth icing that isn't runny. If it looks too runny, add a little more icing sugar to thicken it up. You don't want it to pour off the edges of your cookie.

When the cookies are completely cool, spoon a little white icing onto each one – it's meant to look like a puddle, so don't worry about being too neat. While the icing is still soft, put your marshmallow head in place. Use chocolate chips or chocolate-coated puffed rice for the coal buttons, and place these on while the icing is runny. Leave the icing to harden and set for about 10 minutes.

Once the white icing has set, use the writing icing to draw on stick arms and a nice colourful scarf.

Snowballs

Makes about 24
Prep time: 35 minutes

175g unsweetened
desiccated coconut
2 tbsp runny honey
5–7 tbsp coconut oil, melted
1 tsp vanilla extract

Snowball by name, snowball by nature – these need to be stored in the fridge until you are ready to serve them as they can start to melt a little. They are perfect mouthfuls of coconut deliciousness.

Put the desiccated coconut in the bowl of a food processor and blitz for a few seconds until it forms coarse crumbs. Transfer the coconut crumbs to a bowl and add other ingredients (just 5 tablespoons of the melted coconut oil to start with). Stir with a spoon until you get a thick paste that will hold together when you press it against the side of the bowl. If it's not quite coming together, add a little more melted coconut oil.

Put in the fridge for 20 minutes, until the mixture becomes firm and hardens.

Take it out of the fridge and allow it to come up to room temperature again, so that you can scoop it with a teaspoon.

It will be very crumbly, but press it into about 24 bite-sized balls with your hands – it becomes easier to work with the warmth of your palms. Place the balls on a sheet of baking parchment and store in the fridge until you're ready to eat them. They will melt if they are left out too long, so try to keep them cool (store them in the fridge, in an airtight container – they keep for ages).

Gingerbread Cupcakes

Makes 12
Prep time: 45 minutes
Cooking time: 40 minutes

For the cupcakes:
100g unsalted butter
100g golden syrup
150g self-raising flour
3 tsp ground ginger
150g caster sugar
1 tsp bicarbonate of soda
150ml milk
1 large egg

For the gingerbread people decoration (makes about 30):
75g unsalted butter, softened
75g dark muscovado sugar
1 large egg
1½ tbsp golden syrup
200g plain flour, plus extra for dusting
½ tsp baking powder
1 tsp ground cinnamon
¼ tsp freshly grated nutmeg
¼ tsp ground ginger

For the icing:
300g unsalted butter, softened
600g icing sugar
1 tsp vanilla extract

You will need a 12-hole muffin tin, festive paper liners, a small gingerbread man cookie cutter and a piping bag fitted with a large star nozzle.

I have a real fondness for these. Not just because of the warm, gingery flavours that work so well at this time of year, but because they were the first cupcakes I learnt to ice properly. It is well worth investing in a piping bag and nozzle set if you are a regular cupcake baker, then you can play around with different types of piping. The mini gingerbread recipe makes more gingerbread people than you need for the cupcakes, but that's no bad thing!

Preheat the oven to 180°C/350°F/gas mark 4. Line the muffin tin with paper liners.

Start by making the cupcakes. Melt the butter and golden syrup together in a saucepan over a medium heat. Remove from the heat and leave to one side.

Mix the flour, ginger, sugar and bicarbonate of soda together in a large bowl. Whisk in the milk and egg and slowly pour in the melted butter and syrup, to make a smooth batter.

Pour or spoon the batter into each paper cup in the muffin tin, up to two-thirds of the way up the sides. Pop into the oven to bake for 20 minutes, then take out of the oven and leave to cool in the tin for 5 minutes, before transferring the cupcakes to a wire rack to cool completely (leave the oven on).

While the cupcakes are cooking, make the gingerbread man cookies. Cream together the butter and sugar in a bowl until light and fluffy. Add the egg and golden syrup and combine well, then mix in the flour, baking powder and spices to form a smooth dough.

Dust the work surface with flour and roll out the dough to a thickness of 3–4mm. Cut out gingerbread men with the cookie cutter and keep going until you've used up all the dough (you should have enough dough for about 30), arranging them on lined baking trays as you go.

Bake the gingerbread men in the oven for 10–12 minutes until golden brown, then transfer to a wire rack and leave to cool completely.

Make the icing by creaming the butter in a bowl and slowly adding the icing sugar until the mixture is smooth and light. Add the vanilla extract and beat until smooth. Transfer to the piping bag fitted with a large star nozzle.

Decorate the cupcakes by piping the icing in a swirl on top of each cake, then topping each cupcake with a little gingerbread man.

Mince Pies and Brandy Butter

Makes 3kg mincemeat
Prep time: 30 minutes
Resting time: 2 days

For the mincemeat:
200g stoned dates
200g raisins
100g sultanas
100g currants
100g dried apricots
200g cooking apples
    (1 big Bramley, or
    1½ smaller ones),
    unpeeled
150g walnuts
50g glacé cherries
50g mixed peel
200g shredded suet
    (vegetarian or not)
250g dark muscovado sugar
1 tsp ground cinnamon
1 tsp freshly grated nutmeg
1 large lemon
1 large orange
75–150ml brandy

You will need sterilised jam jars. Either run them through a hot dishwasher cycle and fill them while they're still hot, or wash them in hot soapy water, rinse and dry out for 30 minutes in a low oven (120°C/275°F/gas mark ½). Sterilise the lids in a heatproof bowl with boiling water.

This book wouldn't be a Christmas book without mince pies and they were such a big hit in *Tanya Bakes* that they had to make a repeat appearance. This time around I have given them a bit of a twist by making my very own mincemeat, which I never knew was so easy. When I arrive home at my parents' place for Christmas this is one of the first things I tuck into, with a generous spoonful of Mum's brandy butter on top.

MINCEMEAT

Finely chop or mince the dried fruit – you can use a food processor to do this, but be sure to roughly chop the bigger fruit (dates and apricots) into smaller pieces before adding them to the bowl of the processor, otherwise it will be too chunky. If you've got the time, I'd recommend chopping the fruit by hand to avoid the mixture clumping.

Put the dried fruit in a big bowl. Core and finely chop the apple (skin on) and add it to the bowl of dried fruit. Roughly chop the walnuts, cherries and mixed peel and add them to the bowl too. Toss in the suet, sugar and spices, then grate in the zest of the lemon and orange. Halve the citrus fruits and squeeze the juice into the bowl. Give everything a nice stir to make sure the ingredients are evenly distributed.

Stir in enough brandy to give the mincemeat a moist texture – you don't want to see any of the booze peeking through the mix, but it should all be glossy with a nice coating of juices.

Cover the bowl with clingfilm and leave for 2 days on the work surface (it doesn't need to be in the fridge).

After 2 days, stir the mincemeat thoroughly again and transfer it to sterilised jars, see left (fill the jars as full as you can, to limit the exposure to air). Seal, label and store in a cool place for up to 3 years.

recipe continued overleaf

Makes 12
Prep time: 20 minutes
Cooking time: 20 minutes

340g plain flour, plus extra for
    dusting
110g cold vegetable fat,
    suitable for baking, cubed
60g cold unsalted butter,
    roughly cubed, plus extra
    for greasing
350g mincemeat (see
    previous page for
    homemade)
milk, for brushing
icing sugar, for dusting

*You will need a 12-hole muffin
tin and a fluted round pastry
cutter bigger than the holes of
your muffin tin, and festive
cutters of choice.*

Prep time: 10 minutes

50g unsalted butter, softened
125g icing sugar
1 egg (optional)
50g ground almonds
150ml double cream
40ml brandy

MINCE PIES

Put the flour, fat and butter in a bowl and rub them between your
fingertips until the mixture has a crumbly texture. Drizzle in about
6 tablespoons of cold water, until the mixture comes together to form
a ball of dough. Wrap the dough in clingfilm and chill in the fridge for
30 minutes.

Preheat the oven to 200°C/400°F/gas mark 6. Lightly grease the muffin
tin with butter.

Dust the work surface with flour, unwrap the dough, tip it out onto
the surface and roll it out to a thickness of 3–4mm. Use the fluted round
pastry cutter to cut out 12 circles, each big enough to fit the holes in
the tin.

Press the pastry firmly down into each greased hole and fill with a
heaped teaspoon of mincemeat.

Cut out shapes from the remaining pastry with a festive cutter, such as
a star or Christmas tree, and lay them on top of the pies to form lids.

Using a pastry brush, brush the exposed pastry with milk. Pop into the
oven and bake for 20 minutes or until golden brown. Remove from the
oven and transfer to a wire rack to cool.

Dust with icing sugar and serve with brandy butter. Enjoy!

BRANDY BUTTER

This does contain raw egg, but you can leave it out if you prefer.

Beat the butter and icing sugar in a bowl until creamy, then beat in the
egg and ground almonds.

In a separate bowl, whip the cream until it holds soft peaks, then stir in
the brandy. Fold the cream into the creamed butter-sugar mixture. If not
using immediately, store in the fridge (it will keep for a few days, but
might need re-whipping if the liquids begin to separate). Serve with
mince pies and Christmas pudding.

Christmas Pudding

Serves 8–10
Prep time: 20 minutes
Cooking time: 7 hours (or
    5 hours, plus 8 minutes)

50g self-raising flour
¼ tsp salt
½ tsp ground mixed spice
½ tsp ground cinnamon
½ tsp freshly grated nutmeg
¼ tsp ground cloves
100g shredded suet
    (vegetarian or not)
125g fresh white
    breadcrumbs
75g demerara sugar
50g dark muscovado sugar
100g grated carrot
100g grated cooking apple
    (unpeeled)
150g raisins
100g currants
100g sultanas
50g mixed peel
25g flaked almonds
grated zest and juice of
    1 lemon
grated zest and juice of
    1 orange
1 tbsp black treacle
50ml brandy, plus an extra
    20ml (optional), to serve
2 large eggs, lightly beaten
unsalted butter, for greasing

You will need a 2-pint plastic
pudding basin with a lid.

When I was little, my nanny made this and popped a coin in for one lucky recipient. These days I make it (without the coin), and buy one too, as a treat for my mum when I go back for Christmas. Claridges makes a divine pudding! Traditionally, Christmas puddings are made on the last Sunday in November. The best bit of this tradition is making a dramatic entrance with your pudding set alight and flaming. In our house it has to be served with a big bowl of brandy butter (see page opposite) but you could also accompany it with cream and custard.

Sift the flour, salt and spices into a large mixing bowl. Add all the remaining dry ingredients including the fruit, almonds, lemon and orange zest and mix together thoroughly.

In a small bowl, stir the treacle into the lemon and orange juice as best you can, then stir in the brandy. Finally, stir this juicy mixture into the beaten eggs and tip the whole lot into your big fruity mixture. Stir to combine thoroughly. Cover the bowl with a clean cloth and leave at room temperature overnight.

Grease the plastic pudding basin, including the inside of the lid, with butter. Spoon your pudding mixture into the basin, press it in firmly, pop on the lid and wrap the pudding basin tightly with 2 layers of foil.

Put the foil-wrapped pudding in a large saucepan (you need to be able to put the lid on the pan, too) and bring a kettle-full of water to the boil. Add just enough boiling water to the pan to come half/two-thirds of the way up the side of the pudding basin. Place over a low-medium heat, cover and steam for 5 hours, keeping the water simmering, and remembering never to let the pan boil dry, adding more boiling water as necessary (every 30 minutes or so).

Once 5 hours are up, turn off the heat and, once it's cool enough to handle, remove the pudding basin from the pan. Allow it to cool before unwrapping it from its foil. Store the pudding (in the pudding basin) somewhere cool and dry until Christmas Day.

recipe continued overleaf

On Christmas Day, rewrap the pudding basin in another 2 layers of foil, and repeat the steaming process again, this time for 2 hours. When it's steamed through, allow it to cool slightly, then remove the lid, invert it onto a plate and serve it with brandy butter and a holly garnish.

If you'd like to finish the cooking using a microwave instead of steaming it, be sure there's no foil left on your basin, and lift the plastic lid slightly (so it's not clicked down tight). Microwave on medium power (if you're using an 800W microwave) for 4 minutes. Let it stand for 1 minute with the microwave door open, then cook again for 4 minutes. Leave to stand for another minute, then remove the lid, invert it onto a plate and serve as above.

If you're feeling fancy, ensure the pudding is being served on a platter with a generous rim, remove any holly decoration and measure out 20ml of brandy into a metal ladle. Hold the ladle over a gas flame to heat the brandy and, when it's quite hot, tip the ladle slightly towards the flame (or use a match) to set the liquid alight (if you don't have a gas hob, you can heat the brandy in a small saucepan before pouring into a metal ladle and lighting it with a match). Pour the flaming booze carefully over the pudding and take it to the table. Wait until the flames have gone out before serving.

White Chocolate Winter Wonderland Cake

Serves 8–10
Prep time: 45 minutes
Cooking time: 20 minutes,
   plus chilling

For the cake:
300g unsalted butter,
   softened, plus extra
   for greasing
200g white chocolate,
   broken into chunks
300g golden caster sugar
4 large eggs
350g plain flour
1½ tsp bicarbonate
   of soda
1½ tsp baking powder
½ tsp salt
200ml buttermilk

For the icing:
300g unsalted butter,
   softened
600g icing sugar
1 tsp vanilla extract

To decorate:
icing sugar, for dusting
white ready-to-roll royal
   icing (300g is more
   than enough)
white chocolate stars
   or curls
edible silver glitter
edible silver balls
sparklers (optional)

You will need 3 x 21cm round loose-bottomed cake tins and a snowflake cookie cutter.

If you are not a fan of the traditional Christmas cake (and I know a lot of people who aren't), this is a great alternative. I use my white chocolate sponge recipe as it makes the best celebration cake and most amazing centrepiece. Go crazy with the decorating!

Preheat the oven to 180°C/350°F/gas mark 4. Grease the base and sides of the cake tins and line the bases with baking parchment.

Melt the white chocolate in a heatproof bowl set over a pan of simmering water, making sure that the bottom of the bowl doesn't touch the water, stirring occasionally until smooth. Remove the bowl from the pan and allow to cool slightly.

Beat the butter and sugar together in a bowl with an electric whisk until light and fluffy. Add the eggs one at a time, making sure each one is fully incorporated before adding the next, then fold in the flour, bicarbonate of soda, baking powder and salt. Add the buttermilk and melted white chocolate, and mix to form a smooth, silky batter.

Divide the batter between the cake tins and spread it out slightly with a spatula.

Bake for 20 minutes, or until the cakes are golden and risen and a skewer poked into the centre of the cakes comes out clean. Remove from the oven and leave to cool in the tins for 10 minutes before transferring to wire racks to cool completely.

Make the icing by creaming the butter in a bowl, then slowly adding the icing sugar and beating until smooth and light. Stir in the vanilla extract.

Sandwich the cakes together with one third the icing on a cake stand or serving plate, then spread a very thin layer (another third of the icing) over the top and around the outside to catch the crumbs.

Chill in the fridge for 30 minutes to set the icing slightly, then use the remaining icing to fully cover the cake.

Dust the work surface with icing sugar and roll out the royal icing. Cut out snowflake shapes and stick them carefully to the side and top of the cake. Decorate the top with white chocolate stars or curls, more snowflakes, glitter and silver balls – I also crushed some to scatter around the base of the cake. Serve with sparklers, if using.

Yule Log

Serves 10–12
Prep time: 30 minutes
Cooking time: 10 minutes

For the sponge:
4 large eggs
140g golden caster sugar
60g self-raising flour
50g cocoa powder

For the ganache:
125ml double cream
125g dark chocolate (70% cocoa solids), broken into chunks

For the salted caramel cream filling:
½ x 397g tin of caramel sauce
½ tsp sea salt flakes
300ml double cream

To decorate:
icing sugar, holly sprigs and chocolate shavings

You will need a Swiss roll tin.

I have made a Yule Log every year since I was a little and am a big fan of the traditional chocolate and cream version. Recently, however, I have been experimenting and love the addition of salted caramel to give it a modern twist.

Preheat the oven to 200°C/400°F/gas mark 6. Line the Swiss roll tin with baking parchment.

Start by making the sponge. Whisk the eggs and sugar together in a bowl until light and fluffy. Sift the flour and cocoa powder into the eggs and mix until smooth and combined. Pour into the lined Swiss roll tin and bake in the oven for 8–10 minutes until there is no wobble and the top of the sponge has a nice, light crust.

Turn the sponge out onto a clean sheet of baking parchment as soon as you remove it from the oven and carefully peel the parchment off the base of the sponge. Score a shallow line across the short edge of the sponge, 2cm from the bottom, taking care not to cut all the way through. Roll up the cake tightly, starting from the scored bottom. Leave to cool completely in this position.

While the sponge is cooling, make the ganache. Heat the cream in a saucepan over a medium heat until it starts to bubble at the edges. Take the pan off the heat and add the chocolate, stirring until it has fully melted. Leave to cool completely.

For the filling, put the caramel in a large bowl and add the salt. Mix well. Pour in the cream and whisk until the mixture holds soft peaks.

Carefully unroll the sponge, then spread the caramel cream over it evenly. Carefully roll the sponge up again as tightly as possible without squishing the cream out and leave to rest with the crease at the bottom.

Cut a thick diagonal slice off one end of the log, spread a little ganache over the cut side of the small piece and attach it to the side of the large roll to make a smaller branch (see opposite). Alternatively, leave it as a simple straight log shape if you prefer.

Spread the ganache over the roll with a palette knife, then make lines in the ganache with a fork or palette knife to resemble peeled bark. Finish with a sprinkle of icing sugar and a few sprigs of holly. You can scatter chocolate shavings at the base of the log too, to resemble peeled bark.

Citrus Loaf Cake

Serves 8–10
Prep time: 15 minutes
Cooking time: 30 minutes

170g unsalted butter,
    softened, plus extra
    for greasing
170g caster sugar
3 large eggs
170g self-raising flour
1 tsp baking powder
grated zest of 1 lemon
grated zest of ½ grapefruit
    or 2 clementines

For the citrus drizzle:
150g icing sugar, plus extra
    for dusting
juice of 1 lemon
juice of ½ grapefruit or
    2 clementines

You will need a 1kg loaf tin.

This recipe always makes me think of my family because of our love of the loaf cakes that my mum often makes, but also because of my dad, who can suck on lemons without flinching. I have given this a festive tweak by using grapefruit, which is more traditional around Christmas.

Preheat the oven to 180°C/350°F/gas mark 4. Lightly grease the loaf tin and line the base and sides with baking parchment.

Beat the butter and sugar together in a bowl with an electric whisk until light and fluffy, then add the eggs, one at a time, making sure each one is fully incorporated before adding the next. Fold in the flour, baking powder, lemon and grapefruit or clementine zests, and mix until smooth and well combined.

Pour the mixture into the prepared tin and bake in the oven for 30 minutes or until golden and risen, and a skewer poked into the centre of the loaf comes out clean.

While the cake is baking, make the citrus drizzle. Mix together the icing sugar, lemon and grapefruit or clementine juice in a bowl until smooth and the sugar has dissolved. Remove the loaf cake from the oven, and while the cake is still warm, poke holes into it with a skewer and pour over the drizzle.

Leave the cake to cool in the tin, then turn it out onto a plate and serve, dusted with icing sugar.

Mint Chocolate Mousses

Serves 6
Prep time: 25 minutes
Setting time: at least 3 hours

200g soft-centred mint
    chocolates
250ml whipping cream,
    plus 1 tbsp
2 egg yolks, plus 4
    egg whites
200g dark chocolate
    (70% cocoa solids),
    broken into chunks
70g caster sugar

To serve:
100ml double cream
soft-centred mint
    chocolates, cut into
    shards, to serve

I love mint chocolates whatever the time of year. I wanted to find a way to celebrate them in style at Christmas, and came up with this mousse. It's perfect served in one big bowl for a dinner or chilled in small glasses for bigger parties. I just have to try not to eat all the mint chocolates before I start making it…

Put the mint chocolates in a saucepan with the tablespoon of cream and gently melt over a medium-low heat. Be careful not to let the mixture boil. Remove from the heat when smooth and stir in one of the egg yolks.

Melt the dark chocolate in a heatproof bowl set over a pan of simmering water, making sure that the bottom of the bowl doesn't touch the water, stirring occasionally until smooth. Once melted, stir in the other egg yolk – the mixture will become firm.

Whip the cream to soft peaks in a medium bowl, then separate half the whipped cream into a separate medium bowl. Carefully fold the melted mint chocolates into one bowl of cream and fold the melted dark chocolate into the other.

In a large, clean bowl, whisk the egg whites to soft peaks. Add the sugar, a tablespoon at a time, whisking continuously until the mixture is thick and glossy.

Carefully fold half the egg whites into the mint chocolate cream, taking care not to knock all the air out of the whites. Repeat with the remaining egg whites and the dark chocolate cream.

Spoon the dark chocolate mousse into the base of 6 pudding glasses. Level it out with the back of a spoon, then spoon the mint chocolate mousse on top. Wrap each glass in clingfilm and chill in the fridge for at least 3 hours, or until ready to serve.

Finish by whipping the double cream to soft peaks. Top each glass with a layer of whipped cream and mint chocolate shards.

Mulled Wine, Poached Pear and Ginger Trifle

Serves 10–12
Prep time: 40 minutes
Cooking time: 1 hour,
    plus cooling

For the pears:
750ml red wine (1 bottle)
125g caster sugar
3 cloves
1 cinnamon stick
½ tsp freshly grated nutmeg
1 bay leaf
3 clementines, sliced into
    rounds (skin on)
6–8 conference pears (not
    too ripe)

For the trifle:
250ml double cream
300g ginger loaf, cut into
    2cm chunks
750ml ready-made fresh
    vanilla custard
125g amaretti biscuits,
    crushed
100g toasted flaked almonds
50g crystallised ginger,
    chopped

*You will need a 2-litre trifle
dish (preferably glass, with
high sides).*

This is another pudding that works any time of year but really comes into its own at Christmas. This version most definitely has the wow factor at a feast and works as a great alternative to Christmas pudding. Divine.

Start by poaching the pears. Pour the wine into a saucepan and add 600ml water. Add the sugar, spices, bay leaf and sliced clementines and bring to a simmer over a low-medium heat, stirring until the sugar has dissolved. Leave on a very low heat for about 15 minutes to allow the flavours to infuse. Meanwhile, peel the pears, but leave them whole (stem intact).

Turn up the heat to medium and add the whole pears. Bring to a gentle simmer and poach the pears for 35–40 minutes, until they are deep red and just tender. Carefully remove each one from the liquid and set them aside to cool. Return the liquid to the heat, remove the spices, bay leaf and clementine slices and boil for 15–20 minutes to reduce it by half its volume and create a syrup. Remove from the heat and allow to cool completely before assembling the trifle.

To assemble the trifle, cut your cooled pears in half lengthways and use a teaspoon to carefully remove the core. Trim away the woody stem. Whip the cream in a bowl until it holds soft peaks.

Arrange the ginger cake chunks over the base of your trifle dish. Spoon half of the poaching syrup over the cake, then place the pears around the edges of your dish, with the cut sides facing outwards. Pour in the custard, then sprinkle over the crushed amaretti biscuits. Spoon over the whipped cream and chill in the fridge until ready to serve. Drizzle with the remaining poaching syrup and top with flaked almonds and crystallised ginger, then serve.

Decadent Irish Cream Cheesecake

Serves 8–10
Prep time: 20 minutes
Setting time: at least 2 hours

300g double chocolate
    cookies
100g unsalted butter, melted
450g full-fat cream cheese
100g icing sugar
1 tsp vanilla extract
75ml Irish cream liqueur
200ml double cream
milk chocolate shavings,
    to decorate
whipped cream, to serve

You will need a 21cm round,
loose-bottomed cake tin.

Just yes. Rich and creamy Irish liqueur is the ultimate Christmas indulgence so I had to incorporate it into a pudding. It felt right to combine it with a luxurious cheesecake recipe, and now I have the perfect Girls' Night In dessert.

Put the cookies in a plastic food bag and crush them with a rolling pin until they form crumbs. Tip the crumbs into a bowl and mix in the melted butter until well combined, then press the mixture evenly into the base of the cake tin. Pop it in the fridge while you prepare the rest of the cake.

Mix together the cream cheese and icing sugar in a bowl until smooth, then whisk in the vanilla extract and Irish cream liqueur. Set aside.

Whip the cream to soft peaks in a medium bowl, then fold into the liqueur and cream cheese mixture until combined.

Pour the mixture onto the chilled biscuit base and smooth the top. Chill in the fridge for at least 2 hours. When you're ready to serve, decorate the cheesecake with shavings of milk chocolate, and serve with whipped cream.

Panettone Bread and Butter Pudding

Serves 6–8
Prep time: 20 minutes
Cooking time: 35 minutes

50g butter, melted, plus
    extra for greasing
750g panettone
1 tsp ground cinnamon
1 tsp freshly grated nutmeg
300ml full-fat milk
100ml double cream
2 eggs
100g golden caster sugar
25g demerara sugar
custard, cream or ice cream,
    to serve

*You will need a 30cm oval or
rectangular pie dish or ceramic
roasting dish.*

My heart lifts when I think about bread and butter pudding. It's a warm, stodgy, comforting dish – a hug in a bowl. This time I have made a lighter version using the Italian Christmas classic, panettone cake. You only need half or three-quarters of a cake, which leaves the other half for Christmas Eve.

Grease the pie dish with butter.

Slice the panettone into quarters, then each quarter into roughly 1.5cm-thick slices.

Put a layer of panettone in the bottom of the greased dish, then brush the layer with melted butter. Sprinkle over some of the cinnamon and nutmeg, then repeat the process. Keep going until you have three layers of panettone triangles.

Warm the milk and cream together in a saucepan over a low heat, but don't let it boil.

Whisk the eggs and caster sugar together in a bowl until light and pale, then slowly pour this into the cream mixture over a very low heat, stirring constantly until fully combined.

Pour the custard over the panettone. At this point, preheat the oven to 180°C/350°F/gas mark 4. Allow the pudding to rest while the oven heats up.

Pop the pudding in the oven to bake for 25–30 minutes until the top is golden brown. Sprinkle with the crunchy demerara sugar and return to the oven for a further 5 minutes.

Serve warm with your choice of custard, cream or ice cream.

Chocolate Brownie Traybake

WITH SALTED CARAMEL ICE CREAM

Serves 9
Prep time: 30 minutes
Cooking time:
30–35 minutes

250g unsalted butter,
softened, plus extra for
greasing
200g dark chocolate (60–70%
cocoa solids), broken
into chunks
1 tsp instant coffee granules
300g caster sugar
4 large eggs
(at room temperature)
60g plain flour
pinch of salt
60g cocoa powder
75g white chocolate, broken
into roughly 1cm chunks
75g milk chocolate, broken
into roughly 1cm chunks
salted caramel ice cream,
to serve

You will need a 20cm square
baking tin.

My friend Joe and I ordered this in The Unthank Arms, a pub in Norwich, and it was amazing. It inspired me to create a similar version at home and I think mine is pretty good, too! If this doesn't get eaten in one sitting it lasts well, but I have never had any left over to test that theory.

Preheat the oven to 180°C/350°F/gas mark 4. Grease the base of the baking tin and line it with baking parchment.

Begin by melting the dark chocolate in a heatproof bowl set over a pan of simmering water, making sure that the bottom of the bowl doesn't touch the water. Stir occasionally, and when smooth, add the instant coffee granules. Set aside to cool slightly.

Beat the butter and sugar together in a bowl with an electric whisk until light and fluffy, then add the eggs one at a time, making sure each one is fully incorporated before adding the next. Beat on high speed for 5 minutes, until the volume of the mixture has increased.

Carefully fold the melted chocolate into the butter, sugar and egg mixture, then sift in the flour, salt and cocoa powder. Fold this through with a large metal spoon or spatula, taking care not to lose too much of the air you've beaten into the mixture. Fold in the chocolate chunks, then pour the mixture into the prepared tin.

Pop the tin in the oven for 30–35 minutes, until cooked but still very slightly gooey in the centre. Remove from the oven and leave the brownie traybake to cool slightly in the tin before cutting it into 9 portions and serving it with scoops of salted caramel ice cream.

Pavlova with Mixed Berries

Serves 8–10
Prep time: 20 minutes
Cooking time: 1½ hours

6 egg whites, at room
    temperature
300g caster sugar, plus
    2 tbsp for the fruit
600g frozen mixed berries
3 tbsp Chambord (raspberry
    liqueur)
500ml double cream
1 tsp vanilla extract
edible gold leaf flakes,
    to serve

Any time is a good time for this pudding, but especially Christmas. The white meringue peaks, whipped cream and scattering of berries remind me instantly of a snowy scene.

Preheat the oven to 150°C/300°F/gas mark 2. Line a baking sheet with baking parchment.

Whisk the egg whites with an electric whisk in a clean, dry bowl until soft peaks form (or in a stand mixer fitted with the whisk attachment). Add the sugar a tablespoon at a time, whisking continuously, until all the sugar has been incorporated, then continue whisking for about 6 minutes until the mixture is smooth, thick and glossy.

Spoon the meringue mixture into a large circle on the lined baking sheet, making a smooth circular dent in the middle, and creating whirls at the edges with a spoon or spatula.

Pop into the oven to bake for 1 hour, then switch off the oven and allow the meringue to cool completely inside the oven without opening the door.

While the meringue is cooling, prepare your berries by heating them in a saucepan with the 2 tablespoons of sugar over a medium heat, until the mixture starts to bubble. Allow it to thicken and reduce, but try not to bash the berries too much – you don't want to make a jam. Cook for about 15 minutes, then pour in the Chambord, stir and cook for a further 3 minutes. Remove from the heat and allow to come to room temperature.

When ready to serve, whip the cream in a bowl until it holds soft peaks, add the vanilla extract and whip a tiny bit more. Place the meringue on a serving platter. Spoon three-quarters of the whipped cream into the centre then gently top with the berries. Top with the remaining cream, spoon any syrup from the berry pan over the lot, and decorate with edible gold flakes.

Berry Pie with a Lattice Top

Serves 8
Prep time: 10 minutes
Chilling time: 30 minutes
Cooking time: 50 minutes

340g plain flour, plus extra
    for dusting
110g cold vegetable fat,
    suitable for baking,
    roughly cubed
60g cold unsalted butter,
    roughly cubed, plus extra
    for greasing
600g frozen mixed berries
    (a selection of
    raspberries, strawberries,
    blackberries and
    blueberries work best)
130g granulated sugar, plus
    1 tbsp for sprinkling
40g cornflour
1 egg, beaten
cream, ice cream or custard,
    to serve

You will need a 25cm pie dish.

Preparing this pie makes me feel like Snow White in the cookery scene from the Disney animation. There is something so wholesome and warming about a pie, and the leftovers are great cold for breakfast, too.

Put the flour, fat and butter in a bowl and rub them between your fingertips until the mixture has a crumbly texture. Drizzle in about 6 tablespoons of cold water and bring the mixture together to form a ball of dough. Wrap the dough in clingfilm and chill it in the fridge for 30 minutes. When you pop your pastry in the fridge, take the berries out of the freezer, put them in a large bowl and leave them to sit at room temperature for 30 minutes – you want them to be cold but not mushy.

Preheat the oven to 190°C/375°F/gas mark 5 and grease the pie dish.

Combine the granulated sugar and cornflour in a bowl.

Take the pastry out of the fridge, unwrap it and cut it in half.

Dust the work surface with flour and roll out one of the pieces of pastry into a circle large enough to line and overhang the edges of the pie dish. Line the dish then sprinkle a teaspoon of the sugar and cornflour mixture over the pastry base.

Gently stir the rest of the sugar and cornflour mixture into the berries, then pour the berries into the pie shell. Roll out the remaining pastry to a thickness of 3–5mm and cut it into 10–12 strips, about 2.5cm wide.

Lay 5 of the strips vertically across the filled pie, leaving a gap between each one. Carefully peeling back every other vertical strip to half way. Place a strip horizontally across the middle and unfold the vertical strips again over it. Now, peel back the vertical strips that are underneath the horizontal strip and place a second horizontal strip next to the first one with an even space betweem them. Unfold the vertical strips to cover the second horizontal strip. Repeat this process across the pie until you have a lattice pattern.

recipe continued overleaf

Trim around the edge with a sharp knife or scissors to remove excess pastry, and pinch the base and lattice strips together to crimp around the rim.

Brush the exposed pastry with egg and sprinkle the tablespoon of sugar over the top.

Cover the pie loosely with foil and bake it in the oven for 20 minutes. Remove the foil from the pie and bake for a further 20–30 minutes, until the pastry is golden and the filling is bubbling. If the edges of the crust begin to get too dark before the filling has bubbled, cover the edges with some foil to prevent them burning.

Remove the pie from the oven and serve it warm or at room temperature with cream, ice cream or custard. The filling will thicken as it cools, so if you'd like it to be set a little, let it cool before eating.

Croquembouche

Serves 20
Prep time: 45 minutes
Cooking time: 25 minutes

For the choux buns:
200g unsalted butter
10g golden caster sugar
240g plain flour
8 large eggs

**To fill and assemble
the buns:**
600ml double cream
500g fresh vanilla custard
220g granulated sugar
sparkler, to serve (optional)

*You will need 2 piping bags and
a 1cm nozzle and 5mm nozzle.*

This beautiful pile of choux buns built up in a cone shape, traditionally decorated with spun sugar, originated in France and is one of their most famous celebration bakes. It is a real showstopper, although it is quite an undertaking, especially as it uses hot caramel to glue the buns together, so maybe get an extra pair of hands to help and set aside a whole day – or weekend! I'd probably only recommend this to people who feel they are a confident baker but if you feel you have the skill, it makes for a stunning centrepiece. Here, I have adapted my profiterole recipe and filled them with a custard and cream combination.

Preheat the oven to 190°C/375°F/gas mark 5. Line 4 baking trays with baking parchment.

Put the butter and sugar in a large saucepan with 450ml water and set over a low heat until the butter has melted. Turn up the heat and bring the mixture to a simmer. Take off the heat, quickly tip in the flour and immediately start beating the mixture vigorously with a wooden spoon until a smooth dough has formed. Transfer to a bowl and set aside to cool.

Beat the eggs in a bowl. Slowly add the eggs to the cooled dough in separate, small additions, beating the egg fully into the dough each time, until the dough is smooth, glossy and has a soft, dropping consistency – you might not need all the egg.

Transfer half the choux dough to a piping bag fitted with a 1cm nozzle, then pipe about 30 small balls onto two of the lined baking trays, leaving space between each ball as they will expand in the oven. Re-fill the piping bag with the remaining choux dough and pipe another 30 balls onto the remaining baking trays. Pat the top of each ball with a wet finger so that each ball is smooth.

recipe continued overleaf

Bake the choux in the oven for 20–25 minutes until golden brown and risen. Switch off the oven. Remove the choux from the oven, pierce a small hole in the bottom of each bun with the tip of a knife, and pop back in the turned-off oven for 2 minutes to release the steam from the middle. Transfer to a wire rack to cool fully.

Whip the double cream to stiff peaks in a bowl, then fold in the vanilla custard until fully incorporated. Transfer half the mixture to a piping bag fitted with a smaller, 5mm nozzle. Ease the nozzle inside the hole at the bottom of 30 of the cooled choux buns and pipe in the creamy custard until full. Place the filled choux to one side. Re-fill the piping bag with the remaining filling mixture and repeat with the remaining choux buns.

Put the granulated sugar in a heavy-based saucepan and melt over a very gentle heat. Gently shake or tilt the pan to ensure all the sugar is melting, but don't stir. Continue to cook for about 10 minutes, watching the mixture to make sure it doesn't burn, until you have a clear, golden caramel, then remove from the heat.

Very carefully dip each filled choux bun in the caramel and arrange on a plate, spiralling them up in a cone shape. The caramel will be extremely hot, and will help the buns stick together. If the caramel starts to set in the pan, return it to a gentle heat for just a few moments. When you've stacked all the buns, drizzle the remaining caramel over top and serve with a sparkler in the top, if you like.

Sticky Toffee and Pear Traybake

Serves 10
Prep time: 30 minutes, plus
    20 minutes cooling time
Cooking time: 1 hour

For the pudding:
90g unsalted butter,
    softened, plus extra
    for greasing
160g stoned dates, roughly
    chopped
1 tsp vanilla extract
150g light muscovado sugar
2 large eggs, at room
    temperature
2 tbsp black treacle
175g self-raising flour
1 tsp bicarbonate of soda
100ml milk

For the pears:
5 ripe pears
40g unsalted butter
25g golden granulated
    sugar

For the toffee sauce:
225g light muscovado sugar
100g unsalted butter,
    softened
275ml double cream
1 tbsp black treacle

You will need a 20 x 30cm
baking tray, which is at least
3cm deep.

This is for my favourite person, Jim. Sticky toffee pudding is one of his all-time favourites. Here, I have included pears to give the bake a bit of extra moisture. Serve it with custard, clotted cream or ice cream for an exceptional dessert.

Preheat the oven to 170°C/325°F/gas mark 3. Lightly grease the baking tray and line it with baking parchment. Put the chopped dates in a heatproof bowl and pour over 150ml boiling water. Cover with clingfilm and leave until cold, then add the vanilla extract and mash the dates with a fork – don't worry if it is a little lumpy.

Peel, quarter and core the pears (remove the stems too). Melt the 40g of butter in a large frying pan over a medium heat. Add the sugar and stir until the mixture bubbles and the sugar has dissolved. Add the pears and cook for 5–10 minutes until caramelised and tender, turning them over so that all the sides get nicely browned. Remove from the heat.

To make the pudding batter, beat the 90g of butter with the sugar in a bowl until pale and soft. Beat in the eggs one at a time, making sure the first is well incorporated before adding the next. Add the treacle and mix well. In a small bowl, combine the flour and bicarbonate of soda and add them to the treacle mixture. Gently fold to combine, then fold in the milk. Stir in the mashed dates and their soaking liquid.

Arrange the pear quarters in a layer in the baking tray, and pour over any buttery juices from the pan. Carefully pour the batter evenly over the pears, and pop it in the oven for 45–50 minutes. It's done when a toothpick or skewer inserted into the centre comes out clean.

While the pudding is baking, make the toffee sauce. Gently heat the sugar, butter and half the cream in a large saucepan until the sugar dissolves. Increase the heat to medium-high, stir in the treacle and let it bubble for 2–3 minutes, stirring continuously, until it turns a rich toffee colour. Take the pan off the heat and stir in the rest of the cream.

Allow the pudding to cool in the tray for 20 minutes, then poke it all over with a toothpick or skewer. Pour over half of the toffee sauce, and allow to rest for 15 minutes. Invert the traybake onto a large platter or board to serve, with the rest of the toffee sauce for pouring, and custard or clotted cream or, better yet, vanilla ice cream.

CHAPTER SIX
The Main Event

The Main Event

'Driving Home For Christmas'. This song sums up exactly how I feel as Jim and I head back to my parents' place, the car full of presents, in time for Christmas Eve. The drive home, singing along to snowy festive songs but hoping it doesn't snow until we get there, is the beginning of the holiday for us. It's time to put work to one side and embrace Christmas completely. Being looked after by my mum, surrounded by family and ready to reap the rewards of all the planning is the best feeling.

In this chapter I wanted to take you further into my family Christmas than my Vlogmas videos ever go. I wanted to share with you what happens in our house at Christmas once I have stopped filming. I am sure lots of what we do will be familiar to you and it's a lovely feeling to know how many of us will be sharing similar days wherever we are.

Christmas Eve

Our Christmas Eve has hardly changed since I was a child because we don't want it to! Going out may be a quick trip into town to collect the turkey and pick up any last-minute essentials but really it's an excuse to soak up the atmosphere. In the past, our family would go along to the local church crib service and look at the nativity scene. There would be real animals, including wayward sheep, and we would be encouraged to bring our own pets and join in – our cat Casper would usually get dragged along. Whatever your family traditions, taking a moment out of the house for a breath of fresh air, whether you go for a walk or pick up food orders, is a good idea.

As my sister Tash, brother Oscar and I have got older we are able to help with the final preparations and Christmas Eve baking. We make batches of mince pies and sausage rolls and sing along to Christmas albums, knowing we won't be playing them much longer. We have a glass of sherry, or a big pot of tea and maybe a slice of panettone to keep us going, and when everything is in the oven we collapse on the sofas to watch a film. A family activity, whether it is cooking, playing a board game or choosing a film everyone can watch, is the best way to hang out together.

We don't always cook dinner on Christmas Eve, as the baking and prep for the big Christmas lunch is enough time spent in the kitchen. However, I really want to add to my family's traditions myself and introduce a proper Christmas Eve dinner, a chance to get excited and have a cosy meal before the craziness of the next day. For me, this dinner will be the calm before the storm and I have perfected my Fish Pie (page 198). I love a big dish, made in advance, plonked in the middle of the table with a big serving spoon so everyone can help themselves. And this will give my mum a chance to escape the kitchen and get her last-minute wrapping done.

Before bed there was always a Christmas story and now my dad reads my nephew Isaac 'Twas the Night Before Christmas and I still love hearing it. We put out the same snack for Santa and his reindeer – a carrot, mince pie and glass of milk. Isaac has the best manners and leaves him a lovely letter thanking him for being so kind. Then it's off to sleep where the last thing we all do is hang our empty stockings at the end of our beds…

Silent Night

Michael Haydn

Fish Pie

Serves 6–8
Prep time: 15 minutes
Cooking time: 1 hour
   10 minutes

400g smoked haddock
   fillets, cut into large
   chunks
400g fresh salmon fillets, cut
   into large chunks
250g scallops, trimmed of
   white gristle and red roe
   (if still attached) and
   each cut into 2–3 discs
200g shelled raw prawns

For the cheesy mash:
1kg floury potatoes, peeled
   and halved
50g butter
125g mature Cheddar
   cheese, grated
25–40ml milk
salt and pepper

For the white sauce:
450ml full-fat milk
2 bay leaves
½ onion, peeled
125g unsalted butter
75g plain flour
small bunch of fresh
   flat-leaf parsley, finely
   chopped

You will need a 1.5-litre
ovenproof dish.

I first made this for a Girls' Night In and it was a big hit. When I was doing research while writing this book, I discovered that fish is traditional for Christmas Eve dinner, so I am adopting this as our tradition, too. Make it in advance, pop it in the oven when you are ready, then everyone can gather around and help themselves. Serve with a big bowl of peas or a green salad and do not miss out the Cheddar cheese topping on the mash!

Start by making the mash. Cook the potatoes in a large saucepan of boiling salted water for about 15 minutes, until tender. Drain in a colander, then return them to the pan. Add the butter and 75g of the grated Cheddar and mash until combined. Add 25ml of the milk as you mash, adding a little more if the mash is too thick or clumpy. Season with salt and pepper and leave to one side to cool slightly.

Preheat the oven to 200°C/400°F/gas mark 6.

To make the white sauce, put the milk in a saucepan with the bay leaves and onion and place over a low heat for about 15 minutes.

Meanwhile, melt the butter in a medium saucepan over a medium heat, then add the flour and stir vigorously to combine and form a smooth paste. Cook the paste for a few minutes, stirring all the time.

Remove the bay leaves and onion from the milk and slowly add the infused milk to the butter and flour, stirring all the time. Reduce the heat to low and allow to simmer for 5 minutes before removing from the heat. Season with salt and pepper and add the parsley. Leave to one side.

Pour a third of the white sauce into the ovenproof dish, then add the fish, scallops and prawns. Pour over the remaining white sauce. Spoon the mash over the top and scrape the surface with a fork. Sprinkle with the remaining 50g of grated cheese.

Place the dish on a baking tray and bake in the oven for 25–30 minutes, or until the top is golden and the filling is bubbling. Serve with peas and love!

Christmas Day

Merry Christmas! It really is the most wonderful day of the year. Has Father Christmas been? Has it snowed overnight? Is the oven turned on and ready for the turkey? The first moments of waking are full of childlike excitement. Even now I get the same thrill when I see my stocking bulging at the end of my bed. We don't open our stockings on my parents' bed any longer, but we still have a rule that nobody gets up until after 7am. Like so many families across the country, we all head downstairs in pyjamas and put the kettle on. Everyone dives under the tree for their presents and the levels of noise, music, dogs, squeals of pleasure and wrapping paper are high!

My first Christmas breakfast is often a big mug of tea and a chocolate Santa. My second one a couple of hours later is whatever we fancy, but usually bacon and eggs, croissants and coffee. I take some time out in the morning to have a bath with a *Lush Golden Wonder* bath bomb or some special oils. I tend to dress cosily on Christmas Eve but on the big day I enjoy it more if I make a little effort with my makeup and outfit after an entire morning in my pyjamas. I was the same as a child, and always wanted to dress up on the big day.

When I was little we would go to my grandparents' place – they always made the most incredible roast! Now it's their turn to relax, bring their slippers and come to us for a traditional Christmas lunch. Although I'm not head chef on Christmas Day, I have been perfecting my own roast during plenty of Sundays throughout the year and have kept a note of timings. Whether you are attempting to cook it yourself or helping the person who is, I think this will be an invaluable guide to getting everything on the table.

In the middle of cooking it is easy to forget about laying the table, but it is well worth doing this or asking someone to help you. I think it's nice to make a bit of a fuss with table laying for Christmas lunch, putting out crackers, a centrepiece and all the cutlery and glasses needed. I go into this in more detail later in this chapter with handy tips for how to make your table look extra special. Of course, a turkey with all the trimmings and bowls of roasties and veg also helps!

We always take a break before pudding and play a family game, generally something new that we haven't played before, then it can join the list of family favourites. Jim helps Isaac and Oscar make their toys or they try out a new *Xbox* game.

We head off to Jim's later in the day to celebrate all over again with his family. His sister Nic and brother-in-law Ian are such brilliant, chilled hosts and we arrive to the madness of another big family and Jim's excitable nieces and nephews Ollie, Lily, Harry and Edie. Jim is reunited with his twin John, Sam (Jim's sister) rehearses the quiz and Judy (Jim's mum) is often a little bit merry after even one glass of Champagne! I never think I can eat another thing but when the cheeseboard comes out in the evening I change my mind... We are both very close to our families, and couldn't imagine not spending the day with them, so we are lucky that our families live within 30 minutes of each other and we are able to split the day, alternating Christmas lunch each year.

The Christmas Table

I can't think of anything better than sitting around a table with family and friends, eating, drinking and playing games. At Christmas we spend a lot of time around our table, so making it pretty with candlelight, some festive napkins and a jug of foliage or flowers is a real treat.

On Christmas Day the table is always a hive of activity. We prepare food, build new presents, eat breakfast and chat. Before lunch the table gets cleared and we set it for the feast ahead. This could be laying a freshly ironed tablecloth with matching napkins, a big paper cloth with yuletide motifs that can be instantly thrown away, or you could keep the table bare with a festive runner down the middle. Scattering glittering stars, reindeer and fir-tree confetti instantly turns the table into something magical.

Give the wine and water glasses a quick polish with a tea towel before you put them on the table alongside a big jug of water, maybe with some slices of lemon and a sprig of mint in. Set out the cutlery and make sure everyone has enough so they are not fighting over a fork later. You can buy some really fun paper napkins or lovely white linen ones, depending on your theme, and as an extra touch create foliage place settings as I have done on page 42.

Candles instantly transform a table, and displaying them at different heights adds to the drama. I love a mix of tall candles and tealights but if this is tricky because of little ones then trail some battery-operated fairy lights along the table. You could wind them in and out of greenery decorating the centre. Or put them in a glass vase along with cinnamon sticks and my Dried Orange Slices (page 68). I always want to create an elaborate centrepiece but remind myself how many dishes need to fit on the table and make sure there is enough space for bowls of sauces.

Lastly, you may want to include crackers, although we can't always fit ours onto the table! There are boxes to suit every pocket and the traditional ones are often the best. They turn a decorative table into a social place and make everyone look and feel festive with paper hats, jokes, quizzes and tiny treats.

Christmas Lunch

Although my parents, or Nic and Ian (depending which household we are having lunch in) take the lead on Christmas Day itself, I cook quite a special roast most Sundays throughout the winter months. I feel like I perfect my roast timings more and more every time I make it and I'm excited to share them with you guys as, honestly, timing is everything! I'm so looking forward to when it's my turn to host Christmas one year and I can be head chef!

This is definitely a meal that people have strong opinions on. There is always a debate about whether to include Yorkshire puddings with roast turkey (we always do), what type of stuffing to make, how many vegetable dishes are too many and which sauces to serve alongside. I love how passionate people are about their Christmas lunch or dinner and what they do to make it a success. So much of it is bound up in traditions and influenced by older members of the family. There may be room for a few tweaks, but changing anything substantially can cause uproar! I want a very traditional lunch but am always keen on experimenting with an extra dish of something or an updated version of an old classic.

Here I have given you all of my recipes, processes and a handy timing guide to show you how to pull off the best ever Christmas lunch. I'll admit this does look a little overwhelming and you may decide to do only one or two dishes from this list, which is a good way to start if you have never cooked a roast before. I hope that you can take from the next few pages what you need and feel free to adapt this for your own family and kitchen. Rest assured that I have never cooked this on my own but I get in lots of practice as I love to have friends over for Sunday roasts. I am so excited to finally have this in a book, as it has been in the notes section of my phone for over two years. Part of the fun of Christmas morning is a group vegetable peeling session! Tackle some prep the day before if you can – it makes the morning easier.

As with everything I do at Christmas, creating the right environment to do it in is crucial. Have a clean Christmas-themed apron ready, tune the radio to carols or set up your playlist, give everyone around you a job to do and keep referring to your timings list. Don't panic if things go wrong, take longer or you have to ask for help. The best chefs have a kitchen full of support, including someone taking on the vital role of washing up. Most importantly, cook with love. There is nothing better on

Christmas Day than the moment the last dish has come out of the oven and everyone starts piling up their plates!

SCHEDULE

To eat at 1pm:

08:30 – make sausagemeat stuffing

09:00 – prepare turkey

09:15 – turkey in the oven, start gravy

09:20 – make cranberry sauce

09:45 – peel, boil, drain and roughen potatoes, leave to one side, chop garlic and prepare rosemary

10:00 – prepare and cook the braised red cabbage and the filling for the vegetarian option, then leave to chill

10:15 – remove turkey neck from oven for next stage of gravy

10:30 – prepare the pigs in blankets and carrots

11:15 – put a large pot of water on to boil for the pudding, rewrap it in foil

11:40 – pigs in blankets go in the oven

11:45 – put the Christmas pudding on to steam

11:50 – pop carrots into the oven

12:00 – make Yorkshire pudding batter

12:15 – turkey, pigs in blankets and carrots out of the oven, turn up oven to 220°C/400°F/gas mark 6, heat oil for potatoes and Yorkshire puddings in the oven, roll vegetarian option in pastry

12:25 – put potatoes and Yorkshire puddings in to roast, and the vegetarian option in to bake

12:30 – par-boil cauliflower and broccoli, make cheese sauce

12:40 – cook Brussels sprouts and chestnuts, finish gravy

12:45 – put broccoli and cauliflower cheese in the oven

13:00 – Serve it all up. Cheers!

13:45 – Christmas pudding is ready to serve… if you've got room for dessert!

Christmas Lunch

Serves 8–12

2 tbsp olive oil
1 onion, finely chopped
1kg sausagemeat
75g fresh breadcrumbs
2 tbsp dried sage, or 1
  bunch of fresh sage,
  leaves finely chopped
salt and pepper

SAUSAGEMEAT STUFFING

This may feel a little like doubling up alongside the Pigs in Blankets but every family has their own traditions and this stuffing is very definitely ours. The trick here is to stuff the turkey with it rather than cook it separately – the stuffing can be made and the turkey stuffed the night before and popped back into the fridge.

Heat the oil in a saucepan over a medium heat, add the onion and fry until soft and translucent. Season with salt and pepper, then remove them from the heat and allow to cool slightly.

Put the sausagemeat, breadcrumbs and sage in a large bowl, add the onion and mix everything together with your hands. You can make this a few days in advance and keep it in the fridge, covered, until you're ready to stuff the turkey.

5–6kg free-range turkey with
  giblets
50g unsalted butter, softened
a few sprigs of rosemary
1 chicken or vegetable stock
  cube
50g plain flour
salt and pepper

ROAST TURKEY WITH GRAVY

Where would Christmas lunch be without this magnificent bird? I know other families who choose chicken, duck or goose but we have always had turkey. My parents order it at the beginning of the month and collect it on Christmas Eve. Remember to leave enough space in the fridge to squeeze it in. Make sure the turkey is large enough to feed you all (but small enough that it will fit in your oven) with some left over for sandwiches and for making my Turkey, Leek and Mushroom Pie (page 232). It is well worth spending time on the gravy as there is nothing worse than slaving over a plate of delicious food only to ruin it all by a watery gravy. Here, I give you a meat version only as the Wellington doesn't need gravy.

Preheat the oven to 190°C/375°F/gas mark 5.

If you're using a frozen turkey, take it out of the freezer on the 22nd of December and allow it to defrost in the fridge. When you're ready to cook it, remove it from the fridge to let it come to room temperature,

remove the bag of giblets and stuff the cavity with your sausagemeat stuffing. Pat the outside of the turkey dry with kitchen towel. Rub the butter all over the skin of the bird, then season it well with salt and pepper and tuck the sprigs of rosemary into the creases of the legs. Place it in your biggest metal roasting tin and put the neck of the turkey (from the bag of giblets) in the tray too.

Pour 100ml of water into the roasting tin, being careful not to pour it over the turkey, then pop the whole thing into the oven to cook for 20 minutes per kilo, plus 80 minutes (so for a 5kg bird, the total cooking time is 3 hours), basting the turkey with the cooking juices occasionally.

Put the rest of the giblets in a small saucepan and cover with water. Bring to the boil, then turn down the heat and allow to simmer. Skim off any brown scum from the surface of the water. An hour after the turkey has gone in the oven, remove the neck from the roasting tin and add it to the saucepan with the rest of the giblets. Allow to simmer gently for a further hour, then set the pan to one side.

You can tell when the turkey is cooked because the leg will pull away easily from the rest of the body and the juices will run clear. If you have a meat thermometer, the internal temperature should read 74°C. Remove the turkey from the oven, lift it onto a large board and cover it with foil and clean tea towels for insulation. Allow it to rest for 35 minutes, while you cook the roast potatoes and Yorkshire puddings. Don't panic if everything isn't ready in exactly 35 minutes – the turkey can happily rest for up to an hour.

Finish the gravy by removing the giblets from the saucepan and add the stock cube. Pour any juices from the turkey roasting tin into a jug and allow to sit, undisturbed, so that the fat separates. Carefully pour away as much fat as possible, then pour the remaining juices into the saucepan with the giblet stock. Put the roasting tin over a low heat on the hob and sprinkle the flour over the remaining crusty bits in the tin, using a wooden spoon to stir the flour – these crusty bits are where all the flavour is! Slowly add the turkey stock from the saucepan, stirring all the time to avoid the gravy clumping.

If you don't think there's enough gravy, add a little boiling water from the kettle. Season with salt and pepper and allow to simmer for a few minutes in the roasting tin, before pouring back into the saucepan (if you're not eating immediately) or into a warmed gravy jug to take to the table.

Bring the turkey and gravy to the table for carving. Don't forget to take the sausagemeat out of the inside of the bird and slice it to serve alongside the turkey.

While the turkey is cooking, you can prepare everything else.

HOMEMADE CRANBERRY SAUCE

300g fresh (or frozen, unsweetened) cranberries
grated zest and juice of 3 clementines
3 tbsp sugar

This really is the easiest to make and so much nicer than the shop bought versions. It's a great job to give someone hanging around in your kitchen, or can be made in advance and kept in the fridge. I just have to see a bowl of this and I can instantly taste the roast lunch that goes with it.

Put all the ingredients in a small saucepan over a medium heat. Simmer, stirring occasionally, for about 25 minutes, until the cranberries start to break down and the mixture has a jam-like consistency. Taste it for tartness – it shouldn't be as sweet as jam for toast, but it shouldn't be too sharp! You can either break up the berries gently with a wooden spoon, or stir it more delicately, leaving some berries whole for a chunkier, tarter sauce. Remove from the heat and allow to cool, then store in a bowl or jar in the fridge until ready to use (you can make it up to a week in advance, if you like).

ROAST POTATOES

2kg Maris Piper potatoes (or 1 per person), peeled and halved
100g goose fat (or vegetable oil)
2 garlic cloves, chopped
leaves stripped from 3 sprigs of rosemary
salt and pepper

There is nothing nicer than a big bowl of steaming roast potatoes – crispy edged and fluffy inside – with a sprinkling of sea salt over the top. We often add sprigs of rosemary and a few garlic cloves when we roast ours but we never make them without goose fat. That way you are guaranteed the best texture and taste known to the roastie fan. You can peel the potatoes the night before and leave them in a big pan of water. Drain and replace the water before you boil them. If you're cooking to include a vegetarian at the table, substitute the goose fat for vegetable oil, or make a separate batch of roast potatoes using oil instead of the animal fat at the roasting stage. It works just as well, but isn't quite so Christmassy.

Pop the potatoes in a large saucepan and cover with cold water. Bring to the boil and cook for 10–15 minutes. Drain in a colander, then tip back into the saucepan, put the lid on and give the pan a good shake or two to roughen the outsides of the spuds. You can leave these to one side, with the lid off (so they dry out) until the turkey is out of the oven.

Once the turkey is out of the oven and resting, turn up the oven to 220°C/425°F/gas mark 7. Spoon the goose fat into a large roasting tin and pop it into the oven to heat up for 10 minutes. Remove the pan from the oven and put the potatoes into the hot fat, being careful not to splash yourself. Scatter over the chopped garlic and rosemary leaves, season with salt and pepper, and turn the potatoes in the fat using a slotted spoon. Return the tin to the oven to cook for 35 minutes, or until golden and crispy.

BRAISED RED CABBAGE

1 medium red cabbage, halved, cored and quartered

2 Bramley apples, cored and sliced

1 red onion, thinly sliced

150ml red wine

70ml cider vinegar

80g soft light brown sugar

25g unsalted butter

If you are looking to prepare just a few dishes for Christmas Day, rather than cooking the whole lunch, then I would recommend you try this one. Easy to make, it works well cooked a couple of days in advance and can be reheated with a pile of bubble and squeak on Boxing Day.

Cut the cabbage quarters into thin slices. Put all the ingredients in a big saucepan. Bring to a simmer over a medium-high heat, then turn down the heat to low, cover with a lid and cook for 1–1½ hours, stirring from time to time. Remove the lid and cook for a further 30–40 minutes, or until the cabbage is very tender. You could make this up to 5 days in advance, store it in the fridge in an airtight container and reheat it on Christmas Day.

FOR THE MUSHROOM, SPINACH, PINE NUT AND BLUE CHEESE WELLINGTON SEE PAGE 219.

PIGS IN BLANKETS

10 chipolatas, cut in half crossways

10 rashers of streaky bacon, cut in half crossways

These chipolata sausages wrapped in bacon and roasted in the oven are a non-negotiable part of our Christmas lunch. I always cook more than I will need as everyone has room for extras and they work well cold with a turkey sandwich in the evening. They are also a great additional canapé.

Wrap the chipolata halves in the bacon and place them on a baking tray. You can do this 2–3 days in advance and keep the tray in the fridge until you're ready to cook.

When you're ready, pop the tray into the oven and cook with the turkey for 25–35 minutes, or until the bacon is crispy. Keep warm until ready to serve. You can pop these back in the oven for a short blast of heat as you're dishing up, if you think they need to be hotter before serving.

1kg carrots, peeled, halved
     crossways, then
     quartered lengthways
25g unsalted butter
salt and pepper

CARROTS

Rather unusually, I cook my carrots in the oven with a little bit of butter rather than boiling them. I like the crunch they keep and the buttery sweetness. It also means you save space for other things on your hob.

Put the carrots in a roasting dish, season with salt and pepper, and dot the butter over top. Cover the dish with foil and roast in the oven with the turkey for the last 25 minutes. Remove from the oven and keep warm until ready to serve.

100g goose fat (or 100ml
     vegetable oil if cooking
     for vegetarians)
4 large eggs
160g plain flour
200ml milk

*You will need a 12-hole
muffin tin.*

YORKSHIRE PUDDINGS (MAKES 12)

Yorkshire puddings aren't just for roast beef – they are for turkey too! We love them with any roast as they elevate the meal to another level. They look so glorious puffed up straight out of the oven. Fill them with a good glug of gravy and enjoy.

Divide the fat or oil equally between each hole of the muffin tin, then pop it in the oven for 10 minutes to heat up (at the same time as you're heating up the fat for the potatoes) – you want the fat to be very hot.

Beat the eggs, flour and milk together in a large bowl until smooth (you can make the batter a few hours before you need it, if you like – whisk it again before pouring it into the hot oil). Once the fat is hot, carefully remove the tray from the oven and, using a ladle, spoon the batter into the holes so that they fill each one two-thirds of the way up the cup. Pop back in the oven for 35 minutes. Try not to open the door while the puddings are cooking, otherwise they will sink and lose all their height. Take them out of the oven at the last minute and serve straight away with lots of gravy.

1 head broccoli, trimmed
     and separated into florets
1 head cauliflower, trimmed
     and separated into florets
50g unsalted butter
50g plain flour
450ml full-fat milk
100g mature Cheddar
     cheese, grated
salt and pepper

BROCCOLI AND CAULIFLOWER CHEESE

Combining two vegetables in one dish is a good space saver. We all know how well cauliflower works in a cheese sauce but so does broccoli, and together this makes an appetising side dish. It is also a good recipe to go for if you are not cooking the whole lunch.

Put the broccoli and cauliflower florets in a saucepan, cover with water and bring to the boil. Cook for just 5 minutes, then drain.

Make the cheese sauce by melting the butter in a saucepan over a medium heat. Stir in the flour with a wooden spoon and cook for a

moment, then pour in the milk, little by little, stirring all the time until the mixture is smooth and the milk fully incorporated. Add 60g of the cheese, season with salt and pepper and continue to heat for 5 minutes, stirring occasionally, until the sauce thickens slightly.

Tip the broccoli and cauliflower into an ovenproof dish and pour the cheese sauce on top. Top with the remaining grated cheese and pop into the bottom of the oven for the final 15–20 minutes of turkey roasting time until the cheese is melted. Give them a last blast of heat (with the pigs in blankets) to get the top bubbling. Serve hot.

SPROUTS AND CHESTNUTS

Love them or hate them, sprouts are THE Christmas vegetable. There are all sorts of deliciously clever things you can do with them, but in our family we think you can't beat the traditional addition of chestnuts.

300g Brussels sprouts, trimmed and washed
2 tbsp olive oil
180g whole cooked chestnuts (from a packet), roughly chopped
salt and pepper

While the Yorkshire puddings and potatoes are in the oven, put the Brussels sprouts in a medium saucepan and cover with cold water. Bring to the boil and cook for just 3 minutes then drain in a colander. Set to one side then, when cool enough to handle, cut each one in half from top to bottom with a small knife (if they are big – small ones can be left whole).

Heat 1 tablespoon of the olive oil in a frying pan over a medium-high heat and add the chestnuts. Fry for a few minutes, until the edges are browning slightly, then transfer to a bowl and set to one side. Add the rest of the oil and toss the Brussels sprouts in the pan. Cook for a few minutes, then add the chestnuts back to the pan and season with salt and pepper. Serve hot.

Mushroom, Spinach, Pine Nut

AND BLUE CHEESE WELLINGTON

Serves 6–8
Prep time: 45 minutes, plus
chilling
Cooking time: 50 minutes

600g spinach, washed
30g unsalted butter
1 tbsp olive oil
1 large onion, finely
    chopped
500g chestnut mushrooms,
    thinly sliced
100g whole cooked
    chestnuts (from a packet),
    roughly chopped
2 garlic cloves, crushed
50ml brandy
leaves stripped from 1 sprig
    of thyme, roughly
    chopped
100g pine nuts
180g Stilton (or other
    blue cheese)
500g block of puff pastry
    (ideally all-butter), plus
    1 sheet of puff pastry,
    to decorate (optional)
1 egg
1 tbsp milk
2 tbsp plain flour,
    for dusting
salt and pepper

You will need a lattice cutter
    (optional).

My brother-in-law Ian always thinks vegetarians never get **much of a choice for Christmas dinner so he wanted to create something a bit special for the vegetarians in our family. In his own words: 'I wanted to make something that would still work with all the traditional roast trimmings. The flavours in this Wellington are incredible, and the delicate richness of the sauce and meaty texture from the nuts work really well with the pastry. It's safe to say this always gets prime position on our table!' The filling can be made before the big day and frozen until needed. Make sure it is fully defrosted before you encase it in pastry.**

Bring a saucepan of water to the boil, add the spinach and blanch it for 1 minute, then drain and press as much water out of it as possible. Leave to one side.

Melt the butter with the oil in a large frying pan over a medium heat, add the onion and cook for 3–4 minutes, until softened. Add the mushrooms, chestnuts, garlic and brandy, season with salt and pepper and cook over a medium heat for about 15 minutes.

Stir in the chopped thyme and take the pan off the heat, then tip the mixture into a bowl and allow to cool completely.

While the mixture cools, toast the pine nuts in a dry frying pan over a medium-high heat, tossing them from time to time, until golden brown. Allow to cool before tipping into the bowl with the mushroom mixture.

Once the mushroom mixture has cooled, crumble in the blue cheese, add the blanched spinach, and mix everything together thoroughly.

recipe continued overleaf

Lay a piece of clingfilm about 60cm long on the work surface. Tip the mixture onto the clingfilm and roll it up tightly from one short end, shaping the mixture into a large sausage shape about 25–30cm long, twisting the ends of clingfilm as you go. Place the roll in the fridge for at least 1 hour (or 30 minutes in the freezer).

Preheat the oven to 220°C/425°F/gas mark 7 and line a baking tray with baking parchment. Take the block of pastry out of the fridge 10 minutes before using it, so it can soften slightly.

Beat the egg in a bowl with the milk to make the egg wash.

Dust the work surface with flour and roll out the block of pastry to around 40 x 35cm. Unwrap the roll of filling and lay it along one long edge of the pastry, leaving a 5–7.5cm border at each short end. Gently lift and drape the pastry over the filling, making sure the seam sits underneath the Wellington. Seal the long edges of the pastry with the egg wash, making sure there are no gaps for the filling to run out of as you don't want a soggy bottom! Seal both ends by pressing the pastry together and brushing it with more egg wash, then trim off any excess pastry.

Decorate the Wellington with the leftover pastry or, for a fancy finish, unroll the sheet of puff pastry (let it sit at room temperature for 10 minutes so it's easier to use), roll the lattice cutter over it and gently pull the pastry apart to show the holes, then brush the pastry with the egg wash and place it directly onto the Wellington over the first layer of pastry, wrapping it completely. Glaze with the remaining egg wash.

Put the Wellington on the lined baking tray and pop it in the oven to bake for 30–35 minutes, until the pastry is puffed up and a gorgeous golden colour. Remove from the oven and leave it to cool slightly, then slice and serve.

Boxing Day

And relax. This is the day to eat leftovers, enjoy your presents, stay in your comfies, watch films and play games. It's a repeat of Christmas Day at a slower speed. I have never understood why people want to go sales shopping on this day. I can't think of anything worse than standing in a queue at 5am waiting for the stores to open.

We normally spend the day with Jim's family and eat and drink our way through it. There is always a dog walk and we may pop back to see my family too. Jim's brother-in-law Ian is an incredible chef so he takes control in the kitchen – he is the King of Brunch! I can't resist hanging around the kitchen and helping where I can, although once I managed to break the cork in a bottle of port that Ian had been really looking forward to. Rosie, John's girlfriend, and I couldn't waste it so we found a tea strainer to sieve the port – presentation at its finest! Ian has forgiven me and has even contributed a couple of his recipes for my book. I am thrilled to include his vegetarian Christmas dish of Mushroom, Spinach, Pine Nut and Blue Cheese Wellington (page 219), his Boxing Day Brunch (page 226) and his Palmiers (page 228), as they are absolute winners.

Betwixmas

So you have got through the build-up, the hard work, the fun, the glamour, the excitement and the main event itself. It's lovely to think of all the brilliant crafts, recipes, presents and parties we have made and enjoyed. Now you can really kick back, chill out and enjoy family time. These quiet days between Christmas and New Year are a good opportunity for me to relax. Whether you have to work or not then don't worry, you can still find calm moments. A long bubble bath with a face mask and a good book does it for me every time.

Betwixmas (such a fun new word for those in-between Christmas and New Year days) is all about making it easier for yourself, using up leftovers and turning them into warming dinners (like my Turkey, Leek and Mushroom pie on page 232) or throwing together a super healthy winter salad. You may not feel like cooking at all but often this is the best time to try out a new recipe or experiment with things you find in the fridge. A box of *Celebrations* makes an amazing fridge cake (page 234)! I often make my own pizzas too, using leftover cheese, roasted vegetables, sliced

Top Ten Board Games

Balderdash

Articulate

Scrabble

Monopoly

Cranium

Rapidough

Speak Out

Trivial Pursuit

Taboo

Cluedo

meat, stuffing or red onion marmalade for the toppings. Making pizza dough from scratch is one of cooking's big pleasures and it's so much easier than you think and tastes a million times more delicious than shop-bought bases. It's really therapeutic to make dough on one of those quiet days between Christmas and New Year and it's great fun to get everyone in the kitchen customising their pizzas – you can make it really competitive if you like and award a prize for the best pizza!

Some elements linger throughout the holiday like the games we continue to play, and I have included my Top Ten Board Games opposite if you get a bit stuck. I can't resist a quiz so have written my own festive version that you can try out on your family – I'm known for being extremely loud and competitive, and often end up excitedly shouting out the wrong answer! Or go traditional and set up a 500 or 1,000 piece jigsaw in the corner of the room that you and others can tackle when you need a moment to yourself. We tend to stop watching Christmas films and move on to family classics and any of the good TV dramas that are on.

Getting out for a walk is essential during this time. Wrap up warmly, maybe pack a flask of soup or hot chocolate for longer trips, but get some air whatever the weather. My parents live near the beach so that is always top of our list, but even if you just walk around your neighbourhood you will feel so much better. Then you can flop back on the sofa guilt free!

I do keep in touch with my friends over this time but I am careful about how much I schedule in. It reminds me of earlier in the month when I need moments to be alone and recharge my batteries. Particularly as New Year's Eve is looming and I will need my energy to celebrate!

Boxing Day Brunch

ZESTY AVOCADO, MAPLE-GLAZED BACON AND POACHED EGG ON TOAST

Serves 1
Prep time: 10 minutes
Cooking time: 15 minutes

pinch of salt
1 tsp cider vinegar
1 tsp maple syrup
2 rashers of smoked streaky
    bacon
½ ripe avocado
¼ small Thai red chilli or
    regular chilli
juice of ½ lime
olive oil, for drizzling
2 super-fresh, organic eggs
1 slice of sourdough
1 garlic clove, halved
pea shoots or micro herbs,
    to garnish

I look forward to this brunch all year. It's the first meal after the Christmas Day feasting and made by my brother-in-law, Ian. In his words: 'This is my signature Boxing Day Brunch – the tangy zest of the lime with a little heat from the chilli really works. It brings the avocado to life, plus the extra-crispy bacon gives the perfect crunch to go with the egg yolk.'

Fill a deep saucepan with water and bring it to a rolling boil over a high heat. Add the salt and vinegar.

Heat a griddle pan over a high heat, then brush the maple syrup along the rind of the bacon rashers, put them in the pan and grill on both sides until crispy and charred with grill lines.

Roughly chop the avocado, put it in a bowl and add a small amount of the chilli, half the lime juice and a dash of olive oil, stir gently to combine and set aside.

Turn down the heat under the pan of boiling water. Gently break the two eggs into individual small cups or ramekins, them tip them carefully into the water, one at a time. Turn up the heat to high again and cook the eggs for 2–3 minutes.

While the eggs are poaching, rub your sourdough with the cut side of the garlic clove halves then toast to your desired colour.

Now plate up! Top the toast with the avocado. Lift the eggs from the water with a slotted spoon and drain them on kitchen paper, then lay them on top of the avocado. Pop the crispy bacon rashers in a criss-cross shape on top, drizzle with a little olive oil and garnish with pea shoots or micro herbs.

THE PERFECT POACHED EGG

Discovering the key to perfect poached eggs has been a game changer for me. You don't need to spin the water into a frenzied vortex! Just follow my simple steps above. Remember that fresher eggs will hold their shape better, and the depth of the saucepan and water is important: the deeper the pan the better.

Ian's Palmiers

Each recipe makes 10–12
Prep time: 15 minutes, plus chilling (optional)
Cooking time: 10–15 minutes

For chocolate orange palmiers:
1 ready-rolled puff pastry sheet (320g)
75g orange-flavoured dark chocolate
2 tbsp caster sugar
3 tsp ground cinnamon
1 egg, beaten

For sun-dried tomato and olive pizza palmiers:
8 sun-dried tomatoes in oil (and 1 tsp of the oil), finely chopped
8 pitted black olives, finely chopped
1 tbsp tomato paste
8 basil leaves
1 ready-rolled puff pastry sheet (320g)
100g grated mozzarella
salt and pepper

My brother-in-law Ian makes these as part of our Boxing Day Brunch. 'Yes, they are a treat,' he says, 'but if you can't have them at Christmas then when can you?' Palmiers are the ultimate speedy last-minute pastry and it's easy to involve the kids in making them, too. They can be served up warm in less than half an hour and you can play around with the flavours. Savoury or sweet, they never fail to impress.

To make the chocolate orange palmiers, lay out the sheet of pastry on the work surface, still on the paper it comes with in the packet, and grate the chocolate evenly all over the top.

Mix together the sugar and cinnamon in a bowl, then sprinkle three-quarters of the mixture over the chocolate-covered sheet of pastry.

Lightly roll a rolling pin over the filling to make sure the ingredients are all pressed into the pastry.

Take the short end of the pastry closest to you and roll it firmly and carefully into the centre, and do the same with the other side, so that you have both rolls meeting in the middle. Lightly glaze the roll with the beaten egg. Place it on a baking tray in the fridge for 30 minutes to firm up.

Preheat the oven to 220°C/425°F/gas mark 7 and line 2 baking sheets with baking parchment.

Using a sharp knife, cut the roll crossways into 1cm-thick slices.

Lay the slices on the lined baking sheets, leaving plenty of room between them as they will puff up as they cook. Sprinkle the slices with the remaining cinnamon and sugar mixture and bake for 10–15 minutes. Remove from the oven and leave to cool on the tray. Serve warm.

To make the sun-dried tomato and olive pizza palmiers, put the sun-dried tomatoes, the sun-dried tomato oil and olives in a bowl with the tomato paste, tear in the basil leaves, add a pinch each of salt and pepper and mix thoroughly.

Lay out the sheet of pastry on the work surface, still on the paper it comes with in the packet. Spread the mixture all over the sheet pastry then scatter over the mozzarella and press it into the pastry using the palms of your hands.

Roll, glaze, chill (if needed), cut and bake the pastry as above.

Tanya the Christmas Elf's Quiz

1. How many pipers are piping in the Twelve Days of Christmas?

2. Traditionally, what was included in the Christmas pudding mix?

3. What year was Wham's *Last Christmas* originally released?

4. Tom Smith invented what iconic Christmas product?

5. Where does the candy cane originate from?

6. Other than Rudolph, the most famous of all, can you name five more of Father Christmas's reindeer?

7. How many ghosts visit Scrooge in *A Christmas Carol*?

8. Boxing Day is also known as which Saint's day?

9. Which country gives the UK a Christmas tree for Trafalgar Square each year?

10. What were the children in *'Twas the Night Before Christmas* dreaming about?

11. In Victorian times, what were mince pies traditionally filled with?

12. Which Christmas carol was originally written as a thanksgiving celebratory song?

13. What do the children on *The Polar Express* drink?

14. What is the best-selling Christmas song in the UK?

15. What is the name of the traditional Italian Christmas cake?

16. What was the most likely reason for The Grinch not liking Christmas?

17. Who wrote *The Snowman*?

18. What did Dumbledore give Harry Potter for his first Christmas at Hogwarts?

19. What will Mariah Carey not even wish for in *All I Want For Christmas*?

20. When should the Christmas decorations be taken down by?

1. 11

2. A coin/sixpence

3. 1984

4. Christmas cracker

5. Germany

6. Dasher, Dancer, Prancer, Vixen, Comet, Cupid, Donner, Blitzen

7. Four – Jacob Marley, the Past, the Present and the Yet To Come

8. Saint Stephen's Day

9. Norway

10. Dancing sugar plums

11. Beef

12. *Jingle Bells*

13. Hot chocolate

14. *Do They Know It's Christmas?*

15. Panettone

16. His heart was two sizes too small

17. Raymond Briggs

18. Harry's father's invisibility cloak

19. Snow

20. Twelfth Night

Top Ten Books

Twas The Night Before Christmas - Clement C. Moore

A Christmas Carol - Charles Dickens

How The Grinch Stole Christmas - Dr. Seuss

Little Women - Louisa May Alcott

Letters from Father Christmas - J.R.R. Tolkien

The Tailor Of Gloucester - Beatrix Potter

Starry Night - Debbie Macomber

Let It Snow - John Green

Christmas at Lilac Cottage - Holly Martin

Christmas with Billy and Me - Giovanna Fletcher

Turkey, Leek and Mushroom Pie

Serves 6
Prep time: 30 minutes
Cooking time: 45 minutes

50g unsalted butter
45g plain flour
300ml turkey or chicken
    stock
200g crème fraîche
1 tsp Dijon mustard
juice of ½ lemon
2 tbsp olive oil
1 onion, finely chopped
2 garlic cloves, finely
    chopped
200g leeks, trimmed, rinsed
    and sliced into 1cm
    rounds
300g chestnut mushrooms,
    thinly sliced
450–500g leftover turkey or
    chicken, shredded
1 ready-rolled puff pastry
    sheet (320g)
1 large egg, lightly beaten
salt and pepper

This is the second best thing I would do with leftover turkey, the first best being to pop it in a sandwich on Christmas night. As well as using up the turkey you can add any vegetables lurking in the fridge, but leeks and mushrooms are the perfect partner. I love this pie with chicken instead of turkey, too, at any time of year. And a big pile of mash… You can make the pie filling ahead of time and leave it in the pie dish overnight in the fridge.

Melt the butter in a medium saucepan over a medium heat. Stir in the flour with a wooden spoon and let the mixture cook for a moment. Take off the heat and gradually pour in the stock, then the crème fraîche, whisking all the time, until the mixture is smooth. Return to the heat and bring the sauce to the boil, then turn down the heat to low and simmer for 10 minutes until the sauce thickens, stirring occasionally. Season with salt and pepper and add the mustard and lemon juice.

While the sauce is simmering, heat the olive oil in a large frying pan over a medium-high heat and add the onion and garlic. Stir for a moment, and when the onion and garlic is starting to soften, add the leeks. Season with salt and pepper, then cook for about 5 minutes until the leeks begin to soften. Add the mushrooms, season with a little more salt and pepper, and fry for a few minutes until the mushrooms are lightly coloured and the leeks and onion are soft.

Fold the mushroom and leek mixture into the sauce and add the shredded turkey or chicken, then pour into a pie dish. Allow to cool.

When ready to cook, preheat the oven to 200°C/400°F/gas mark 6 and take the puff pastry out of the fridge to soften slightly. After 10 minutes, unroll the pastry on the work surface and cut it to fit the top of your pie dish. Place it on top of the dish, crimp the edges with your fingers, and make some decorations with the leftover scraps of pastry. Brush the top with beaten egg.

Pop the pie in the oven and bake for about 30 minutes, until the pastry is shiny and golden. Remove from the oven and allow to rest for 5 minutes before serving.

Chocolate Heaven Fridge Cake

Serves 12
Prep time: 15 minutes
**Setting time: at least
    2 hours**

200g double chocolate
    cookies
100g unsalted butter
150g milk chocolate, broken
    into chunks
150g dark chocolate (70%
    cocoa solids), broken into
    chunks
150g golden syrup
150g chocolates, unwrapped
    and roughly chopped
25g mini marshmallows
60g roasted hazelnuts,
    chopped (optional)

*You will need a 20cm square
baking tin.*

**This is ridiculously easy to make, low on effort but off the
scale on chocolate! It's the perfect way to use up a box of
chocolates or any random sweet treats and biscuits. It lasts
well in the fridge and can be pulled out at any moment if a
surprise guest pops by.**

Line the baking tin with clingfilm, leaving extra clingfilm hanging over
the sides.

Put the cookies in a plastic food bag and crush them with a rolling pin
until they form rough chunks.

Melt the butter, milk chocolate, dark chocolate and golden syrup
together in a heatproof bowl set over a pan of simmering water, making
sure that the bottom of the bowl doesn't touch the water, stirring
occasionally until smooth.

Remove the bowl from the heat and add the crushed cookies, chopped
chocolates, marshmallows and hazelnuts (if using).

Scoop the mixture into the lined tin and press it flat with a knife or
spatula. Leave the mixture to cool at room temperature then chill in the
fridge for at least 2 hours.

Invert the cake onto a board and peel away the clingfilm. Cut into
12 pieces.

CHAPTER SEVEN
Happy New Year

Happy New Year!

So here we are at the final chapter of the book and the final day of the year. I always feel a bit sad that Christmas is well and truly over but I am already dreaming about what I want to do in the year ahead. There are mixed emotions about saying goodbye to the year gone but so much excitement about welcoming in the new one.

I love to go out and party but I don't expect it to be the highlight of my social calendar. I think there is a lot of anxiety around how you spend New Year's Eve, so don't feel pressured. The important thing is to celebrate the coming year exactly as you want, whether that is a big bash or a night in (I have mentioned various ideas in this chapter to help you decide). I adore going out but I think my favourite New Year's Eve is being with Jim, my closest friends and family. There is nothing better than delicious food, a glass of Champagne, a group countdown and hugging and kissing everyone you love at midnight!

Waking up on the 1st January I always feel the thrill of a new start and want to spend the day embracing that. In our family we have traditions similar to those on Christmas Day but way more relaxed. Continuing these customs really helps me to start the year how I mean to go on.

So, new year, new you? Well wait just a minute! What's wrong with the current you? We are always so ready to assess our failings and look at what we need to improve without taking a moment to congratulate ourselves on what we have achieved. Take the time to think about what you are grateful for and how far you have come over the past year. If the year hasn't gone as well for you as you would have wanted, then now is a good opportunity to reflect. I have written a little about this too, so I hope it is some help.

Happy New Year!

New Year's Eve Celebrations

Here are some ideas of how to celebrate.

* Throw a party – OK, so this takes the biggest effort but can also be the most rewarding. Some people say that only the brave host a party on this night because of the expectation attached. Ignore that, read my chapter about organising a bash and do it!

* Going to a party – As much as I love to host a party, attending someone else's is always so much fun and obviously a lot less pressure!

* Go to your local pub – Most pubs organise an event. It's a great way to get all your friends together without someone taking responsibility for hosting. The nicest thing about being at the pub is that there will probably be a buzzy vibe already there you when you arrive, which is nice for you and your friends to bounce off! It's also a really fun way of making new friends, and you don't know where the night will take you.

* A dinner party – A more intimate way of celebrating with friends, and a lovely way to spend the day, cooking and getting ready. You could take the pressure off by asking everyone to bring a course or contribute something. As I mentioned earlier in the book, the best dinners end with us dancing around the kitchen or on our chairs, balancing precariously!

* Take a break – Booking a little cottage somewhere in the country and going away with your friends is a brilliant way to enjoy the time without pressure. Everyone is together to chill out, cook and celebrate, and it is the perfect antidote to a family-heavy Christmas.

* On the sofa – Sometimes this is the best place to be. Just because you decide to stay at home doesn't mean you miss out on celebrating. Invite everyone who is on the sofa with you to get into their pyjamas, order a takeaway and open a bottle of Champagne. Maybe watch a film, but remember to switch on the TV to see the Big Ben countdown and watch the fireworks over the River Thames.

Reflecting on the Year Gone

There is always an end-of-year moment to reflect and think about the good and not so great times during the year passed. It is important to celebrate what you have achieved over the last 12 months and to recognise how far you have come. They don't have to be big milestones: think about the small things that have made you happy and times when you have been proud of yourself. It is important to congratulate yourself and enjoy those successes.

So, what happens if your year hasn't gone so well? There will always be good and bad parts to every year – it is just how life unfolds – but sometimes it can feel a bit relentless if you've been experiencing more of the latter. We all have hitches, suffer from anxiety or struggle at times. The close of a year is the perfect opportunity to take stock and look at any worries you are facing. Asking for help is a big step in the right direction. Find someone you trust to talk to – I don't necessarily mean a professional but a good friend, parent or partner. It's amazing how saying something out loud can immediately make it feel less scary. Your listener may also be able to suggest a way of solving or coping with the problem that you hadn't thought of.

Sometimes it's the little things that trouble us, the moments of anxiety that catch us unawares. At this point I try to remember how much I have to be grateful for and how lucky I am. I also think it is important to be extra kind to yourself when you feel your spirits dipping. Take some time, space and quiet to recharge, have a break from social media for an evening, take a long soak in the bath and an early night with a book that you can completely escape into. It works for me every time.

I have friends who use rituals around this time of year. It can be a cathartic and positive way to move forward. My favourite is to write troubles and worries on pieces of paper. Depending on who you are with, you can read them out loud or just repeat them in your head. Then, either rip or shred the paper up or throw it onto a fire. It is the perfect excuse for lighting a winter bonfire in the back garden! Or, you could write a letter to yourself talking about what you hope to achieve over the next 12 months. Put it away somewhere safe but allow yourself to refer to it six months in. That way you can check you are on course and amend anything you need to before you look at it the following New Year's Eve. It's a good way to see how far you have come in a year and how much you have achieved and resolved.

Traditionally, this is the time to make resolutions for the year ahead. I try not to get caught in the frenzy of writing a list of things I want to do and change that are unrealistic and will only make me feel bad about myself when I don't achieve them. By the same token, I do like to set some goals and attainable targets as this makes me feel really motivated. Last year I vowed to sign up for a run, but I knew aiming for a half or full marathon was just going to overwhelm me and I needed to manage my expectations. I decided on a 10k and with training and commitment I did it. The sense of accomplishment was worth the hard work!

New Year's Day

New Year's Day is a quieter, calmer version of Christmas Day for me. Wherever I am I make sure my day is just as delicious, and I have traditions that make it special. Breakfast is always a bacon sandwich accompanied by lots of coffee. It's a slow start to the day after a party night!

As children, we would head straight to the beach, and I still try and meet my parents there for a New Year's Day walk. Wherever you live, whatever the weather, try to get out for a walk because it is a wonderful way to kick-start the year. Walking along the beach, wrapped up, wind whipping around us, waves crashing, and breathing big lungfuls of icy air. The dogs go mad. Strangers greet each other. We blow the cobwebs of the past year and a late night away in an instant. It's a great way to talk about our plans for the year ahead and share any resolutions we have made. Then we each have a '99' ice cream and get one especially for the dogs so they all get a lick.

Back home the house smells of the baked ham that has been cooking since we left and everyone is starving after being in the fresh air. Side dishes are much simpler than Christmas Day's festive fare: jacket potatoes, a crunchy winter slaw and an enormous jar of tongue-tingling pickled onions. We all sit down to a big lunch with a lot less fuss than the week before. Then it's games, snoozing on the sofa, watching films and trying not to mention or think about the return to work. All over for another year…

New Year Ham

Serves 6–8 (with leftovers)
Prep time: 15 minutes
Cooking time: 4 hours
    45 minutes

4–5kg boneless gammon
    joint
5 cloves
1 cinnamon stick
1 tbsp black peppercorns
2 bay leaves (fresh or dried)
1 orange, halved
4 tbsp marmalade

This is our traditional New Year's Day lunch. There's nothing better to come back to after a breezy beach walk to welcome in the new year than a ham, with jacket potatoes, winter slaw and pickled onions. It also makes a great Christmas Eve dinner.

Place the whole gammon joint in a large pot and cover with cold water. Add the spices, bay leaves and orange halves and bring to the boil. Boil the gammon for 4 hours, occasionally skimming off any scum that rises to the top. Turn off the heat and allow the ham to cool slightly in the liquid before carefully lifting it out and transferring it to a board. Save the stock to use in soups or other recipes (it will freeze well).

Preheat the oven to 200°C/400°F/gas mark 6.

Carefully remove the top layer of skin from the ham, leaving as much of the fat underneath as possible. Score the fat in a criss-cross diamond pattern. Place the ham in a large roasting tin. Heat the marmalade gently in a small saucepan for about 4 minutes, until just runny, then brush the marmalade all over the ham. Bake in the oven for 25–35 minutes, or until the glaze is golden and the fat crisp in places. Leave to cool a little, and serve in slices or chunks.

JACKET SPUDS

6–8 medium Maris Piper
    potatoes (one per person)
butter, to serve

Preheat the oven to 200°C/400°F/gas mark 6.

Wash and dry the potatoes – the drier the potato, the crisper the skin. Prick all over with a fork so that they don't burst in the oven. Put the potatoes directly on the oven shelves and bake for 1 hour, or until soft – you can check this by inserting a knife into the fattest bit of the biggest potato; if it goes in easily, they're done. Remove the potatoes from the oven and serve with lots of butter.

WINTER SLAW

1 medium white cabbage,
    finely shredded
1 red onion, thinly sliced
25g bunch of chives,
    finely chopped
4 carrots, peeled
3–4 heaped tbsp
    mayonnaise
salt and pepper

While the potatoes are baking, make the slaw. Put the cabbage, onion and chives in a large bowl. Using a vegetable peeler, peel the carrots into long ribbons and add them to the bowl. Season with salt and pepper, then spoon in 3 tablespoons of the mayonnaise. Toss the salad in the mayo and check the consistency – if you like your coleslaw creamier, add some more mayonnaise.

Goals For The Year Ahead

❋ MINDFULNESS – This may be an overused word but don't let that put you off. Meditation, in whatever form, gives you time to stop. It creates a space for you to concentrate on your breathing and clear your head. Try ten minutes every morning before your day starts. I have lots of apps on my phone to help me with this as I don't have the discipline to do it myself. I also find that exercise really helps. You don't need to join a gym, if that's not your thing. Why not go for a walk every day, run around the park, swim outdoors or try yoga if you never have? Anything that calms your thoughts and gives you that natural buzz after you have exercised is worth it.

❋ BALANCE – In the past I have spent the weekdays focused on healthy eating and exercise then got to Friday and collapsed into indulgent dinners and TV-watching sofa weekends that would carry on for days and healthy weekdays would go out of the window! There is room for both but I knew I needed more consistency and bigger periods of time between treat days, so I could feel amazing for longer. I really struggled with this so I made it a big goal at the beginning of the year. I now feel properly on top of it and am actually quite proud of how far I have come! So, I think this is a much better target for the year ahead than taking up a crazy diet or extreme exercise routine and not being able to keep it up past January! It has

worked for me so I hope it does for you too. It also helps to look at other areas of your life where you need a little more balance, maybe in work or relationships.

❊ PHONE OFF – We are all guilty of being stuck to our phones, using them for so many reasons in various situations a hundred times a day. Finding a balance with this can be really difficult but there are moments in the day which give you a good opportunity to take a break from your phone. When you meet a friend for a catch-up, talk to them without checking your phone every five minutes.

Don't eat dinner with your phone on the table. Leaving your phone downstairs when you go to bed or at the opposite end of your room means you are less tempted to take a final scroll through social media. Don't let it be the last thing you do at night or the first thing you do when you wake up.

❋ TAKE UP A HOBBY – Maybe there's something you have wanted to learn but are not confident enough or are lacking in time. I started learning the piano at the age of six but stopped as a teenager, so my plan is to have a weekly lesson. There are also evening classes where you can learn just about anything. Or write a little list of things you want to find out about and teach yourself via the power of books and the internet. I always have a list of books I want to read, too. It is the best form of escapism and the perfect way to relax. Put together a list of ten books you would like to read throughout the year and remember to include a couple of classics in there, too.

❋ SEE YOUR FRIENDS – This may seem like a silly thing to put on your list, but how often do you spend proper quality time with your friends, without screens and other interruptions? January can be such a depressing month, so invite them over for tea and cake. After all the fun of December, nobody wants to spend any money, so think of other things to do together like helping each other clear out your wardrobes! My friends and I do this a lot, as well as cooking together or tackling a crafty project. Thinking about the year ahead, perhaps you could all plan a trip away either overnight to a lovely hotel or book a little cottage in the country. I love having a treat with my friends to look forward to.

❋ HELPING OTHERS – This could be in tiny ways by donating to a charity of your choice, taking part in a sponsored event or organising a cake sale. I definitely want to carry on trying to help and raise awareness about lots of issues that I feel passionate about. Let's all try and make more of a difference in the year ahead.

✷ GIVE THANKS – For the little and big things in your life. Stop and think of them and be grateful. There are always things you can be thankful for – you don't need to make a list of them, just hold them in your head. Never take anything for granted. Ever.

Index

Picture Credits

Cover images and food, craft and fashion photography by David Munns, excluding pages 35 (top right, bottom left), 66

Cover images and portraits on pages 5, 7, 14, 17, 26, 35 (top right, bottom left), 54, 59, 67, 74, 95, 103, 140, 192, 238 by Dan Kennedy

Cover images and images on pages 22, 25, 55, 83, 129, 130, 132, 134, 136, 143 (top), 197, 247 by Amber-Rose Smith

Additional photography by Tanya Burr with the exception of those appearing courtesy of:

Shutterstock: 61 (bottom right), 236-237

Stocksy: 12-13, 15, 19, 31, 52-53, 60 (top right), 61 (top left, top right, bottom left, middle right), 72-73, 77, 81, 82, 98-99, 100, 138-139, 143 (bottom left, bottom right), 190-191

Watercolour illustrations by Irina Vaneeva/Shutterstock

Acknowledgements

There are lots of people I need to thank for making this book so magical...

My exceptionally hardworking and amazing team, Kate, Lucy, Georgia and Millie, who put up with my Christmas-related texts and phone calls not only in February, but also at 3am when I'd wake up with a sudden worry about the book or realisation that I'd used the word festive five times in one paragraph.

The wonderful people at Blink publishing and the brilliant creative team Kelly, Laura, Emily, Lucy, Alex, David, Ian, Dan, Sam, Adam, Alan and Gillian.

The enormously supportive and truly lovely people who have been following me over the years and are only ever a tweet away.

My family: you guys are the reason I love Christmas so much. Thank you for always making it the most special time every single year and giving me the most incredible childhood memories ever. I wouldn't have been able to do this book without you.

My friends, for all the fun festive times over the years and not complaining when I invite you over to a Christmas photo shoot at my house on the hottest day of the year and make you sit in front of the smokiest fire pit there ever was.

And of course, Jim, thank you for making every Christmas since we've been together more and more special each year. I don't know how you do it and I just think you are the best.